W9-DFE-754

ALBERT REYNOLDS
The Longford Leader

The Unauthorised Biography

Tim Ryan

BLACKWATER PRESS

Acknowledgements

I wish to express my thanks to the many people who helped me bring this book together.

In particular, I wish to thank the *Irish Press* library, the National Library, Derek Cobbe, Norman and Olive Spence, John Cooney, Maurice Manning, Michael McDowell S.C., Eugene McGee, editor of the *Longford Leader*, and John McGee, assistant editor of *Business and Finance*. I am indebted to Paddy Cole for his help on the ballroom era and to Aidan Kellegher for the historic note on the Mac Rannaill clan.

May I also thank the many people who generously gave their time to be interviewed. Their names appear throughout the following pages.

Finally it was, as always, a pleasure to work with John O'Connor, editor Deirdre Greenan and the team at Blackwater Press.

Editor
Deirdre Greenan

Design & Layout
Paula Byrne

ISBN
0 86121 549 4

© Tim Ryan 1994

Produced in Ireland by
Blackwater Press, c/o Folens Publishers
8 Broomhill Business Park, Tallaght, Dublin 24.

Dedication

To the memory of the late Senator Willie Ryan – farmer, community worker, politician and friend.

About the Author

Tim Ryan is a political reporter with the *Irish Press*. A graduate in Latin and English from University College, Cork, he was a teacher before entering journalism. He is the author of *Mara* (1992) and *Dick Spring, A Safe Pair of Hands!* (1993). He is currently writing a biography of musician Paddy Cole.

Contents

Introduction

St Patrick's Day, 1994. The venue: the White House in Washington, and the occasion: the St Patrick's Day Banquet. President Bill Clinton, who had earlier received the traditional bowl of shamrock from Albert Reynolds, was delighted to host the Taoiseach as chief guest of the evening.

The entertainment was Irish too. Derry composer and musician, Phil Coulter, who had flown in specially for the function, was seated at the piano.

'I feel thrilled to be in the presence of two great men,' began Coulter. 'I couldn't help remarking to myself that both of our distinguished leaders here have more than a passing knowledge of the music business.

'It's pretty common knowledge that Mr President, in his teenage years, had to make a decision between becoming a musician and a politician, while our esteemed Taoiseach was a very prominent promoter of entertainment in Ireland for many years. So I couldn't help thinking that if fate had dealt a slightly different hand of cards, tonight I could be the supporting act in the Point Depot in Dublin on the opening night of Albert Reynolds' promotion of the first leg of the sell-out tour of Bill Clinton and his Arkanas Blue Birds.'

The crowd erupted in laughter as Coulter launched into *Boulevogue.*

The comparison of the two leaders was striking. As he tucked into the main course of traditional lamb chops and Irish stew, Albert Reynolds could delight in the fact that Irish/American relations were at an all time high.

He had the firm support of the US Administration for the recently signed Downing Street Declaration, which had enormous potential to break the deadlock in Northern Ireland.

That support was set to underpin the breakthrough in securing the September 1994 IRA ceasefire, the high point in Albert Reynolds' political career.

His simple, unaffected, country background helped Reynolds to form a close relationship with British Prime Minister, John Major, a relationship that would never have been possible, for example, between Charles Haughey and Margaret Thatcher.

While a backbench TD and Government Minister, Reynolds had never shown very much interest in the North. However, as soon as he was elected Taoiseach in February 1992, he pledged to give the seventy-year-old problem his undivided attention. While the Tánaiste and Minister for Foreign Affairs, Dick Spring, was given nominal responsibility for the North, Reynolds was involved with every move.

His close contacts with John Hume and Reynolds' perseverance, which often left him isolated, finally led to the long-awaited IRA ceasefire on 1 September, 1994, ending twenty-five years of bloodshed in Northern Ireland.

'If I never did anything else, I would be happy,' declared a delighted Taoiseach who celebrated by breaking a lifelong teetotaller pledge to sip a glass of champagne.

A few days later, on Tuesday 6 September, a proud Albert Reynolds engaged in a historic handshake with the President of Sinn Féin, Gerry Adams, and the SDLP leader, John Hume. The event signalled the dawn of a new era in the efforts to resolve the problems of the North.

A leader who once declared himself a 'one page man' Albert Reynolds was an unlikely Taoiseach and, at first glance, would appear to have been far more at ease running ballrooms, something he did very successfully in the 1960s.

The contrast between Reynolds and his predecessor, Charles Haughey, could not be more striking, even in the minor details of his personality. Reynolds is, for example, persistently late for appointments, something which was anathema to Haughey. Reynolds is generally late because he can't stop talking to people.

Having received a good secondary education at Summerhill College in Sligo, the young Albert Reynolds decided to abandon academic life and try his fortune as an entrepreneur.

He first worked at a variety of jobs in CIE and Bord Na Móna before he finally found his niche in running dance-halls in the early 1960s. That is, until the money-spinner came to an abrupt halt following a disagreement with his brother.

But he had caught the bug of being an entrepreneur and quickly became immersed in a most colourful career which saw him run a bacon factory in the heart of Dublin's Liberties, export salmon and lobster to Paris, open a cabaret centre, own a local newspaper, until finally he joined in partnership in a petfood business, now controlled by the Reynolds family.

Politics was something Albert Reynolds had little time for in his early years. His first introduction to the world of conspiracy and intrigue was through Independent Dáil Deputy Jim Sheridan, for whom he acted as Director of Elections.

But once bitten by the political bug, Albert Reynolds dislodged the sitting Longford Fianna Fáil TD, Frank Carter, and was on his way to Leinster House and Government Buildings. Later he said that his main political influence was the late Seán Lemass. Asked in 1989 if the Lemass economic philosophy – that a rising tide lifts all boats – still held, Reynolds replied: 'Yes, to a very large extent'.

In Longford Reynolds and Fianna Fáil are the major political force.

'Everything that happens in the area is alleged to have come from Fianna Fáil, including the by-pass and the sewage scheme, things that clearly would have come anyway,' says Eugene McGee, the editor of the *Longford Leader*.

McGee, who once ran the rival *Longford News* for Reynolds, is amused at his transformation since he became Taoiseach.

In particular, he smiles at the poetry contained in the many speeches made in foreign cities which arrive on his desk. He keeps a sample of them close to hand, and entertains callers to his office by quoting some of the poetry. When he talks in Longford, Reynolds – who can still give a spirited version of *The West's Awake* – throws the civil service speeches away, and talks off the top of his head.

To the casual observer Albert Reynolds can appear to be a very straightforward, honest, no-nonsense politician. In the words of Eugene McGee: what you see in Albert Reynolds is what you get – almost!

But behind the bonhomie and the camaraderie is an intensely clever politician. Ever alert, and helped by the fact that he is a teetotaller, Reynolds is listening, planning and executing political moves twenty-four hours a day, seven days a week.

As a businessman he has enjoyed moderate success. While many of the ventures he became involved in failed, he successfully pioneered the family petfood business from its early unstable existence to its current position as a major employer in the Midlands. Those who were in business with him say he was tough and ruthless.

But history will judge Albert Reynolds not as a businessman, but as a politician. It is still far too early to make any real assessment of that role. However, his role in helping to bring about the IRA ceasefire has secured him his place in the history of the twentieth century.

The following pages tell the story of the making of Albert Reynolds, from his days as a young boy by the river Shannon in Rooskey to the lofty heights of the Taoiseach's office in Government Buildings . . . and to his historic handshake with the President of Sinn Féin, Gerry Adams.

Chief of Muintir Eolais

Like former Taoiseach Charles Haughey, Albert Reynolds can claim close kinship with at least three counties. Now generally regarded as a Longford man, he was born in Roscommon, but his roots are in County Leitrim.

There, in the valley of Gortletteragh, an area known in the Middle Ages as the Feadha Chonmaicne (Woods of Conmaicne), lay one of the principal seats and fortresses of the Mac Rannaills (Reynolds is the anglicised form), chiefs of Muintir Eolais, on the shores of Loch Rinn. In addition to a fortress on the lake, the Mac Ranaills had a castle on its shore, then known as Caisleán Lecce Deirge, the remains of which can still be seen.

The clan originally sprang from Raghnall, an ancient warrior of the Conmaicne sept. The family roots can be traced back both to the Ulster Kings of the line of Ir, son of Milesius, and also through Queen Maeve of Connaught, sons of the Kings of the line of Hermon. From the latter they inherited their territory in Muintir Eolais which was part of South Leitrim enclosed in the diocese of Ardagh.

In 1247 both the crannóg and castle were attacked by MacGosdell (Costelloe), who came from beyond the Shannon and expelled the chieftain, Cathal Mac Rannaill. However, with the assistance of the O'Connors, Mac Ranaill was able to recover the crannóg and break down the defences of the castle on the shore.

The Mac Ranaills owned territory very close to the O'Rourkes to whom they were obliged to pay customary dues. They often rebelled, sometimes with limited success, but generally sustained heavy losses. These Gaelic tribes were engaged in bitter squabbling at a time when the Anglo-Normans were busily capturing the better lands in Ireland.

The following extracts from the *Annals of the Four Masters* highlight the anarchy of the period:

1306 AD Farrell Mac Ranaill, Chief of Muintir Eolais, was slain by his brothers and a party of his own people.

1314 AD Mahon Mac Ranaill, Chief of Muintir Eolais, O'Mulvey, Chief of Muintir Cearbhalainn, and many of their people were slain by Mulroney Mac Dermot, Lord of Moyburg.

1345 AD On his way back from Loch Rinn, where he had gone to the assistance of Mac Ranaill, Tordhealbhach O'Connor, King of Connaught, was killed with an arrow at Guirtín Na Spideóige in Fidh Doruidha (now Feadaro) in the parish of Annaduff.

The first mention of whiskey in Irish history is recorded in the *Annals* under the year 1405, when it is stated that a certain Ristéard Mac Ranaill, heir to the chieftainship of Muintir Eolais, died on Christmas Day from a surfeit of *aqua vitae*!

1430 AD Brian, son of Tiernan Óg O'Rourke, was slain by the sons of Maolaghlin Mac Ranaill at Maelhail.

From the year 1468 Muintir Eolais were divided. In that year Cathal Óg died, and was succeeded by Tadhg Mac Ranaill while Sliocht Mhaolsheachalinn elected William Mac Ranaill as chieftain. William and his clan had their headquarters at Loch Rinn, while the legitimate chieftain established his base further north at Loch Scurnear, Keshcarrigan. William died at Loch Rinn around 1473. There was constant warfare between the two groups until 1474 when the legitimate chieftain was given the submission of the rival clan.

Thomas Mac Ranaill (from the Loch Scur clan) was the first Reynolds to abandon the Irish name around 1560. This was during the reign of Queen Elizabeth l, and he became known as Mac Ranaill Galda (the English Mac Ranaill).

Thomas was succeeded by the notorious Seán Na gCeann (Seán of the Heads) who was noted for his cruelty to prisoners, whom he beheaded for little or no reason. He was the first Reynolds to abandon his faith and embrace Protestantism.

There was much criticism of this move and in order to stifle it he invited all the leading chiefs of Muintir Eolais to a banquet at Loch Scur Castle which he built in 1570. As was the custom they came unarmed, but Seán and his men set them up and they were all murdered.

In 1612 he is mentioned as keeper of His Majesty's jail for County Leitrim. In 1660 the family owned some 10,000 Irish acres of land which comprised all of South Leitrim, part of Roscommon and part of Longford. However, they lost most of this during the Clanwilliam Plantation.

The family had abandoned Loch Scur Castle by the end of the eighteenth century, but George Nugent Reynolds lived nearby at Letterfine. The blind harper, Turlough O'Carolan, was a regular visitor to his 'Big House'. While there Reynolds told the harper some of the Fianna legends of the two Queens who once lived on the neighbouring hills of Sí Bheag and Sí Mhór, and the disputes which often occurred between them. Carolan pondered the legends and after some days came up with his first known music composition 'Sí Bheag, Sí Mhór'.

George Nugent Reynolds was killed at the 'Sheemore Duel' by Robert Keon in 1786.

And so ended the privileged position of the Mac Ranaill family – that is, until Albert Martin Reynolds became Taoiseach of the Republic of Ireland 206 years later in 1992.

–1–
The Tuck-Shop King

February 15, 1992. A bitterly cold evening in Longford Town. Yet thousands of people made their way to a platform erected over the tourist office on the town's Main Street.

Homecomings are always special occasions, particularly in rural Ireland. Normally it is the local football or hurling team that is to be accorded the honours. But this was a very special homecoming. Local hero Albert Reynolds had been elected Taoiseach of the land. The euphoria was palpable.

From the moment he crossed the county bounds, people thronged the route. There were crowds in Edgeworthstown where the petfood factory which Albert Reynolds helped to start is located. He visited the Manor Nursing Home where many of his seven children were born. All along the route bonfires blazed to mark the return of the new chief.

As the moment of the Taoiseach's arrival in Longford Town drew near, the platform became overcrowded when more VIPs than expected turned up. The Bishop of Ardagh and Clonmacnoise, Dr Colm O'Reilly, who lives in the town, had to be squeezed in when he was spotted in the crowd.

Mayo man Pádraig Flynn, the new Minister for Justice, got a helping hand from a few burly Gardaí onto the platform too. There, also, was another new Minister, Brian Cowen, and old-hand John Wilson.

Another familiar face, Senator Seán Doherty, was easily recognisable, as were Senators Paschal Mooney, Seán Fallon, Michael Finneran, Brian Mulooly, Donie Cassidy, Terry Leyden and many others. Close friend for many years, Senator Eddie Bohan had travelled down from Dublin for the occasion.

MC for the evening, Ned 'The County' Reilly, was in top form although a trifle nervous before such a large crowd. A keen sportsman in his youth, he would have felt easier displaying his skill as a footballer many years before.

Ned introduced the 'lesser acts' and warned them to keep their contributions short. Then came the moment for which they all waited. 'Now ladies and gentlemen,' said Ned, 'it is the proudest moment of my life to introduce Taoiseach na hÉireann, Albert Reyno...'

The roar of the crowd took over before he could finish. The echoes must have been heard in Rooskey, the tiny village in nearby Roscommon where Albert Reynolds was born sixty years previously.

The new Taoiseach spoke without a script for over half-an-hour. It was a mixture of thanks to the local people, without whose support he would never have had the opportunity of getting elected in the first place, combined with some thoughts on wider, national issues. He recalled his 1977 nomination for the Dáil in the Courthouse when John Scanlon from Granard and Mickey Doherty successfully put his name forward.

Albert Reynolds spelled out the three Es that would dominate his leadership – Efficiency, Effectiveness and Enterprise.

'We must root out the waste in Ireland,' he declared. 'And we need the ordinary people to come with us. Governments cannot do everything themselves.'

Referring to the North, he said it would be ironic if, when all the barriers in Europe were coming down, Ireland would be seen as the last outpost of rancour and division.

On his new Cabinet he said they would work as a team.

'As a captain I know you will expect me to lead that team well.'

The only emotional moment in his speech came when he referred to his wife Kathleen who was not on the platform, although she was present later in the Longford Arms Hotel. Albert Reynolds was visibly moved as he mentioned Kathleen's illness – she had cancer – and her recovery.

He concluded by telling the audience that some of the locals now had a problem as to how to address him – Albert or Taoiseach.

'I don't care what you call me, call me anything you like,' he said. 'So long as you support me when I need support, that will do me fine. Together we will do it for Ireland in Europe.' The crowd roared with approval.

Albert Reynolds' appointment as Taoiseach had been secured following his election as leader of Fianna Fáil at a Parliamentary Party meeting on 7 February.

The resignation of Charles Haughey as Taoiseach had been an anti-climax, and Albert Reynolds had quietly moved into the top job.

But the new Taoiseach had come a long way in his sixty years. The former dance-hall manager had tried his hand at numerous projects, some of them rather daunting, before concentrating in the end on politics, a move that surprised even his closest relatives.

Albert Martin Reynolds was born in the village of Rooskey in Co Roscommon on 3 November, 1932. For reasons still unclear, his date of birth repeatedly appeared as 1935 on Dáil records until he finally set the record straight in the Dáil in 1993.

Wishing him a happy birthday in the house on 3 November of that year, Fine Gael Deputy Austin Deasy asked Mr Reynolds to clear up a matter that had been bothering deputies and people outside the House for a number of years.

'Are you fifty-eight, or are you sixty-one?' asked Deasy. 'And Ted Nealon wants to know for his book.' This was a reference to the fact that up to then Nealon's *Guide to the Dáil* put Albert Reynolds' date of birth as November 1935, which would have made him fifty-eight at that time.

The Taoiseach replied that he wished to give his correct age, 'For once and for all, and for the record – sixty-one'.

Located on the banks of the Shannon, just off the main artery to the West, Rooskey is a picturesque little village surrounded by hills.

'My earliest memories of Rooskey are of a good rural environment, the friendliness of the people there, the annual Shannon Regatta and the flow of farmers taking their animals to Hanley's Meat Factory,' Jim Reynolds, Albert's brother, told the *Longford Leader* in 1992.

Albert Martin Reynolds was born the youngest of a family of four. His father, John P Reynolds, owned a small piece of land and combined his farming with coach-building and undertaking. He later converted the coach-building shed into a small ballroom on the shores of the Shannon.

'My father was an unusual man for that time in that he saw business potential,' recalled Jim Reynolds. 'He had great entrepreneurial flair, although that word was not used at the time. He was an auctioneer, an undertaker, a transporter, and was, of course, a farmer.'

Dance-halls were a business the young Reynolds were familiar with from the time they were old enough to hold a sweeping brush.

'You know the way smells stay with you?' Albert said years later. 'I'll never forget the smell of the paraffin and stuff called 'Grano' we used to have to polish into the floor so that people could glide across it.'

Albert's mother was Catherine Dillon from Clune in nearby Co Leitrim. She had been to America and was on a visit to her sister, who had married a Bowen in the village of Rooskey, when she met John Reynolds. Catherine Reynolds was deeply religious and gave her family strong values, a sense of purpose and a work ethic.

'Growing up we learned the value of family life, hard work, and the value of prayers,' said Jim Reynolds.

Pakie and Catherine Reynolds had three sons – Joe, Jim and Albert, and a daughter, Teresa. The family lived on the Main Street in

Rooskey, opposite the old courthouse. The eldest of the family, Joe, still lives there. Jim was later to go into business with Albert, while their sister, Teresa, kept the Reynolds name all her life as she married a man called Charlie Reynolds. She is now a widow, but lives in the area. The family were not at all political and the topic was rarely discussed in the home.

'I suppose you could say we were a Fianna Fáil house,' eldest brother, Joe, later recalled. 'At election times in Roscommon my mother and father would always vote for Gerry Boland and Dan O'Rourke, 1 and 2 in that order.'

Joe's first memory of the young Albert was his amazing capacity to reel off the names of horses from playing cards.

'There was a man called Jimmy Kelly lodging in our house in the late 1930s. He was the first man to be employed at Hanley's bacon factory next door. He had hundreds of those cards with horses.

'When Albert was about two years old and could just about talk a bit, he could name every single one of those horses. Jimmy Kelly would try to puzzle him, but no matter which way he would turn and twist the cards, Albert would get the name right. It was an amazing sight.'

As a schoolboy, Albert Reynolds' pals were the Hanleys who lived nearby, notably Seamus and Peter (Peter was to remain a lifelong friend); Master Caslin's boys, Thomas, Louis and Noel; and the sons of Garda Cronin.

Another neighbour, May Hanley, who still lives in the village and then owned one of the local pubs, remembers Albert as a youngster.

'I remember him as an altar boy in the church,' she recalls. 'He seemed to be a leader even at that time.'

Later she would do business with him when he would buy hot meals from her for the showbands coming to the Cloudland.

Albert Reynolds began his schooling at the local Rooskey National School, but his mother heard of a great teacher, Elizabeth McLoughlin at Carrigeen, four miles outside Rooskey.

Elizabeth McLoughlin was twenty-six when she took over the one-teacher school in Carrigeen in 1942. Albert was one of forty-five pupils in her classes which were divided from infants up to sixth class. As was the case in hundreds of small schools around the country, she would give a number of classes exercises to complete while she taught the remainder herself. It was difficult, but she managed to secure a number of coveted County Council scholarships for her students.

Albert Reynolds came to her too late for a County Council scholarship, but she put him forward for a 'Burse' to Summerhill College in Sligo.

Today she can still remember him and his mates in the class of '45, among them Monsignor Kevin Flanagan, now living in New Jersey.

'Anything I would ask him to do, he would get it done,' she recalls. He was 'very determined and a good mixer'.

Albert cycled to school from Rooskey each morning and brought the newspaper to his schoolteacher. In Carrigeen Ms McLoughlin taught the budding Taoiseach Maths, Irish, English, History and Geography. Albert was intelligent and learned quickly.

Elizabeth McLoughlin taught all subjects through Irish and as Albert was weak in the subject, she brought him to her own home nearby for tuition on Saturdays.

Questioned by journalists in Dublin's Jury's Hotel on the day of his election as leader of Fianna Fáil, Albert replied: 'Tá beagán agam. Níl Gaeilge líofa agam. Táimse chun feabhas a chur air'.

When the examinations were complete in June, there was still some time before the school closed for summer holidays in July. Elizabeth McLoughlin used this time to teach her pupils a little French and Latin, and to introduce them to Shakespeare. In Albert's year she introduced the class to *The Merchant of Venice*. Perhaps the young Albert picked up his first hints on business from Shylock, the crafty Jew.

Today Carrigeen National School is boarded up and the people of Rooskey are hoping for a new school in the village.

But Albert Reynolds had won his bursary and was off to boarding school in Sligo.

Summerhill College was, in effect, the diocesan seminary for the diocese of Elphin. Many of the students went on to study for the priesthood at colleges like Maynooth or Kiltegan. Some would return as priests to teach in the college, or to work in the diocese.

As well as boarders, there were a number of day pupils who provided a vital food supply line to the inmates. The Second World War had ended, but rations were the order of the day for a time.

'It was in boarding school in the rough days when the food wasn't great and you got no visits, that I learned to look after myself,' Albert Reynolds said later.

'*Estote Factores Verbi*' (Be Ye Doers of the Word), taken from the Epistle of St James, was the motto of the school where the Classics, Greek and Latin, received a high priority on the syllabus. The teachers were strict but fair.

'You'd often have the tops of your fingers taken off,' Albert recalled.

Fr Charles Kelleher, later President of the College, taught Irish.

Joe Jennings, former Government Press Secretary and currently a Departmental Information Officer, but then a pupil in the class ahead of Albert Reynolds, can still recall the fear of the boys when Fr Kelleher would send out for a cane to administer punishment. Fortunately, he generally selected a thick stick which inflicted less pain on the hands. Fr Kelleher also trained the College football team.

Another priest, Fr Thomas Foy, now living in Nazareth House in Sligo, taught English, while Fr Kevin Dodd was nicknamed 'Failed Maths' because of his ability to put even the most dense student through their exams.

Writing in the College *Annual* of 1951, Michael Devine, who was also a year ahead of Albert Reynolds, and now a priest in the United States, wrote: 'I remember the wild dash to the radio after tea on

Sunday evenings to get the day's sports results. I remember the joy of utter laziness in sitting under the shade of the trees on the Long Walk and watching the more athletic-minded contending in the sunshine. I remember the hustle and bustle of going home, and I remember the quiet beauty of the evening devotions and the strong boyish voices raised in praise of Our Lady, in the *Litany of Loreto*.'

One of Albert Reynolds' classmates in Summerhill was his childhood friend, Gerry Casey, now a Ford dealer in Castlebar. He recalls him as a 'good mixer and a very practical fellow, able to talk to anybody and everybody's friend'.

Summerhill was basically a GAA College, but Albert Reynolds hung around with a soccer crowd and played rugby and table tennis. The sports section of the 1951 College *Annual* states: 'There was plenty of mud on all pitches this year and among those who enjoyed the sticky going during the rugby season were A Reynolds (scrum-half)...'

'He was bright-eyed and bushy-tailed,' recalled Paschal Morrison, a student during Albert Reynolds' time, and now with An Post in Sligo. Another classmate, Fr Dominic Gilhooly, recalls Albert as being 'friendly with everybody'.

Fr Gilhooly remembers Albert as being among a few exceptional students of the Classics, and his Latin and Greek exercise books were always in great demand.

'He was able to use ablative absolutes when we'd be resorting just to infinitives. Fr John Feeney was our Latin and Greek teacher. He used to go around the class and test us on our knowledge of the various constructions we had been asked to translate. Invariably he would say: "Mac Ranaill, déan iarracht air". And while Albert would protest that he had done it not so long ago, Fr Feeney insisted that he do it again. Albert might only have the air of the thing, but he always managed to give such a convincing performance that he was commended for his efforts.'

'He was a great guy who had his wits about him. If he got bread from home, he'd know where to get butter,' recalls Joe Jennings, who shared the same dormitory as the future Taoiseach. 'You might hear him at night shuffling about, getting some cake out of a suitcase.'

Albert's mother regularly visited her son in Summerhill, sometimes staying in a guesthouse in Sligo for a night or two.

'There was little money around in those days. She would take a parcel of cakes and bread to Albert and maybe take him out of College to Gray's Cafe on the bridge in Sligo for a feed,' his brother Joe recalled.

But Albert Reynolds was already showing entrepreneurial skills. He began to 'bulk buy' sweets for the College and sell them at a profit.

'You had a loose couple of shillings. You'd go down the town, buy maybe six bars of chocolate and a few bags of sweets and you'd sell them to the guys at a small profit so that you had your own for nothing,' he told Deirdre Purcell in a *Sunday Tribune* interview.

The College authorities spotted the aptitude for commerce, and appointed him to take charge of the school tuck-shop. He bought the goodies from Bergin's Wholesalers in the town and made a tidy profit for all concerned.

'The school didn't keep the money,' he said. 'They put it back into, say, improving sporting facilities, that sort of thing.'

In Summerhill Albert Reynolds' interest in dancing already began to manifest itself. Another classmate, Seamus Creighton, penned a short piece about him in the College *Annual*:

'Albert Reynolds – one of the finest table-tennis players in the house . . . a fine billiards and snooker player, has won many competitions . . . his main hobby is dancing . . . has danced to most of Ireland's leading bands, and Albert's decision on the merits of a band may be always regarded as final . . . a most likable personality . . . our able tuck-shop manager. . . his ambition: to become a teacher.'

Seamus Creighton went on to become a distinguished academic priest and studied in Rome. But tragically, while going to answer a doorbell in Summerhill College on 1 November 1965, his foot caught on his soutane. Fr Creighton fell and hit his head against the wall, breaking his neck. He died later that day.

Another friend in the class of '52 was Fr Niall Molloy, who later died in mysterious circumstances in a house in Clara, Co Offaly.

Meanwhile Albert Reynolds was pursuing his studies. In the 1949 Summerhill *Annual*, extracts from students' essays include, under the heading '*Flights of Fancy*', the following: 'Little by little the clouds began to screen the blue sky from our view. *A Reynolds.*'

Under the headline '*November*' the 1951 *Annual* records the following: 'Bookshops are flooded with books and Christmas cards, and even the country people begin to brighten their houses for Christmas. For the countryfolk, November is a lazy month. The farmer relaxes after a hard year's work to admire his sheds packed with hay and turf and his barn full of threshed corn. At night the neighbours gather into one house and talk the long night away. The children are often frightened by the ghost-tales of the old people and, retiring to bed, sleep the night with their heads under the blankets. *Albert Reynolds.*'

At holiday time Albert Reynolds returned home to Rooskey. But his brother Joe recalled that he had little interest in work:

'I remember he hated working on the outside. We had a beautiful horse-drawn hearse and a bit of a field at the back. I drove the horses. Albert never did, he couldn't stick them.

'He would even dodge the haymaking when we'd be piling the ricks. You could always find Albert at the bottom of our field where the Shannon flowed, swimming in a place we called "The Canal". Joe Egan, the Caslins and the Hanleys would be racing across the river with him. It was a safe place and he was a very good swimmer.'

But Albert Reynolds' ambition to be a teacher was dashed when he broke a leg during his Leaving Certificate examinations in June 1952.

However, he attained honours in three subjects, Irish, English and Greek and passed others. He never collected his results from Summerhill until they were finally presented to him by the current President of the College, Fr Kevin Earley, on a *Bibi Baskin Show* on RTE television in September 1991.

– 2 –
Mr Taylor's Advice

Albert Reynolds left Summerhill College at the end of the school year in 1952 without any idea what he would do for a living.

'I don't regret having finished at Leaving Cert – that was back in the '50s,' he said later. 'It is a changed world since then. We are living in very different times.'

He thought about a career in banking and went for an interview and a written examination in Dublin.

'At lunch-time, before the afternoon exam, I saw some of the other applicants walking around the grounds of O'Connell's Schools with the interviewers from the previous day. So I said to myself: "This is not for me." And so I didn't bother doing the exam. I left and bought the evening papers and looked through them for job vacancies.'

Subsequently, the bank wrote to Albert's parents enquiring as to why he hadn't sat the examination, having impressed the interviewing panel. Not only was the bank surprised at his sudden lack of interest in a banking career, so too were his parents.

He took his first job in a hardware store in numbers 43 and 44 Pearse Street in Dublin. JC McLoughlin's was a hardware emporium which was situated next door to what is now Mahaffy's public house. His wages were £2/10s per week. After paying for his keep in Lower Mount Street he had only a half-crown left. However, help was at hand. His older brother, Jim, who worked as a carpenter with the young PV Doyle's building company, earned £25 a week and occasionally gave Albert some extra cash. After a short time Jim emigrated, first to Canada, and later to Australia.

While working in JC McLoughlin's Albert claims to have picked up a piece of advice he has never forgotten.

'I was an office assistant. The old man in charge of the office, Mr Taylor, asked me what I was going to do. At the time I was answering the telephone, doing messages, licking stamps on envelopes and bringing the post down to the local sorting office. Mr Taylor said to me: "Young man, if you don't think where you are going, you'll be licking stamps for the rest of your life. It is not a question of being someone, but rather choosing to do something, and doing it better than anyone else." It was the best advice I ever got, I have never forgotten it.'

After Jim Reynolds emigrated, the young Albert Reynolds got a job as a cabinet polisher in the PYE radio factory in Dundrum.

He soon decided to study accountancy at night.

'While I stopped formal structured education after Summerhill College in Sligo, I studied accountancy up to final exams in my first few jobs,' he told *The Irish Times* in 1987. 'I self-educated myself as I went along because that was a time when a lot of parents couldn't afford university education. I developed as I went along.'

He sat the examinations for Bórd Na Móna and CIE, the secure places of employment at the time.

He was offered, and accepted, a job as a clerk with Bórd Na Móna at Ballydermot, Co Offaly, where his wages were now £3/10s per week.

'There wasn't much excitement around Ballydermot, I can tell you,' but, characteristically, he noticed, while compiling the accounts, that Bord Na Móna's custom of renting turbary to local families was potentially lucrative. He took a plot of turf himself and found that by working every second Saturday and part of every second Sunday, he could earn an extra £5 per week. At the same time he was continuing with a correspondence course with the School of Accountancy in Glasgow, passing all his examinations as far as Intermediate stage.

By now Albert Reynolds had decided that he would not be a clerk with Bord Na Móna for life either. Mr Taylor's advice was still ringing in his ears.

'At Bórd Na Móna I saw the fellow with the B Comm employed as the accountant, and the manager was an engineer. From my reckoning I was going to be a clerk for the rest of my life, and again I decided it wasn't for me.'

His next chance came with the offer of a permanent post with CIE. He was sent to Dromod, Co Leitrim, two miles from his own home in Rooskey. He took up the job on 27 April, 1953, as a Clerical Officer (Grade 3) on a salary of £227.13s.0d per annum. He continued to study accountancy, and got the first part of his final examinations.

His job with CIE involved organising delivery sheets for lorries and booking goods forward on trains. In Dromod one of CIE's customers was the local Lyons meat factory. There Albert was to come across a man, Matty Lyons, with whom he would later go into partnership in a petfood factory.

Over the next few years Albert Reynolds transferred to Ballinamore, Drumshambo, Ballymoate and Longford before returning to Dromod.

Denise Rogers, later personal assistant to Employment and Enterprise Minister, Ruairi Quinn, grew up in Ballymoate near the railway station, and can still remember the young CIE goods clerk, Albert Reynolds.

'We used to cross the railway line as a short cut to get from one place to another,' she recalls. 'This was against the rules of course, and Albert used to chase us with a brush!'

Another woman, then a very young girl in the town, who remembers the CIE clerk, is Olive Braiden, later Director of the Rape Crisis Centre and a Fianna Fáil candidate for the European Parliament in the June 1994 election. Her family ran a hardware store in the town.

'My memory of Albert is of him going up and down from the station to his lunch every day,' she says.

Ballymoate was to be a fateful posting for Albert Reynolds as it was there he first met his wife, Kathleen.

Kathleen Coen was working in McGettrick's outfitters on O'Connell Street, when Albert Reynolds arrived as the new CIE clerk. Today Kathleen is still remembered in the town as 'a very nice girl with a terrific amount of character'.

Kathleen and Albert met through their jobs. Goods for the Ballymoate drapers arrived by train, and who else to deliver them but the goods clerk. Payment was normally made by Kathleen.

'I couldn't help noticing what a handsome chap he was when he came into the shop,' her former boss, Martin McGettrick, recalled.

'Some of the girls used to be making faces at Albert behind his back, when he was talking to Kathleen. Albert was so shy, and I would come and stand there until he was uncomfortable and then go. But I didn't nip it in the bud, anyway.'

While working in Ballymoate Albert Reynolds stayed in lodgings for three years with Mrs May Hunt of Wolfe Tone Street. There were twelve or fourteen staying there, so it was quite a houseful. Along with her husband, Pat, Mrs Hunt provided full board for all of them and, with four children herself, catering for twenty people every day was hard work.

Occasionally Kathleen's brother, Paddy, stayed in the boarding house and Albert and Kathleen would meet there. Albert and Paddy Coen became pals and sometimes went dancing – Albert's favourite hobby – together.

Limerick businessman Nicholas Jackman, husband of former Fine Gael Senator, Mary Jackman, also stayed at Hunt's when in the area. He remembers Albert Reynolds as a very shy, retiring fellow.

'Albert was very quiet and sincere and not at all like the fellow you sometimes hear him made out to be today,' he says. 'I was friendly with Paddy Coen who worked in the Post Office and he used to stay there as well. It was a very good home and often visiting actors such as Jimmy O'Dea and Danny Cummins stayed there. Albert was always very well turned out, I remember that well.'

May Hunt can still remember the night love blossomed between Albert Reynolds and Kathleen Coen.

'One night they were going to a dance – I think it was Victor Sylvester – a few miles away. One fellow worked in the courthouse, and he had a car. Seven or eight of them went off to a dance in the car and Kathleen went too – and that was that.'

Young Albert had no car yet and instead he and Kathleen used to go off cycling together.

They got married in the early '60s by which time Albert had left CIE. But he still keeps in touch with Mrs Hunt.

'Albert would often call when he was in Ballymoate to see his in-laws,' she told the *Longford Leader*. 'He called me himself and invited me up to Dublin on the day he was elected Taoiseach.'

As the new Taoiseach was walking along the corridors of Leinster House, being congratulated and shaking hands with numerous well-wishers, he caught sight of his old Ballymoate landlady.

'Well, I see May Hunt,' he declared. 'And are you still giving the good dinners?'

His delighted former landlady summed him up as 'a grand lad who loved a game of cards'.

A significant mark in Albert Reynolds' life was when he took on the job of secretary of the Rooskey Carnival Committee in 1955/56. He had become involved with the committee 'doing all the work that was usual in a country parish'. More importantly, he was the one responsible for booking the bands and the marquee.

'You learned to have the booking done six months in advance, to have it well organised,' he recalled. He liked the dancing game, booking the bands, manning the box, wheeling and dealing. It was the perfect antidote to the comparatively boring tasks of a country CIE clerk.

The young entrepreneur ran the marquee successfully for two years, helping the parish priest to pay off a debt. During the third year the priest came to him and said, 'My church is built, my debt is paid, I've enough money collected. That's it Albert, thanks a lot.'

However, Albert had other plans. He had already made advance bookings and given commitments, but he didn't have the money.

'I asked a brother of mine (Joe) to come in with me, and we decided to do it ourselves.

'I ran the marquee for two years. It was very successful. During the second year my brother, Jim, came home from Australia. We sat down and discussed the whole business. We were all single. It looked like a good opportunity.'

Running dances was not entirely new to the family. Their father had had a small dance-hall years earlier at the back of the family home.

The budding Taoiseach enjoyed the atmosphere of organising dances. As the business grew he managed to hold on to his day job, still invoicing away for CIE under the benevolent eye of a particularly enlightened station master, Dominic Leyden, who told him that as long as the work was done on time, he did not care when Albert actually did it.

'And,' said Albert, 'I reckoned I could do the job comfortably in three hours a day . . . it's a principle I have consistently applied myself.'

But the next station master, Brendan O'Meara, did not take the same flexible view. 'He tried to change my whole lifestyle.'

Young Reynolds was bluntly told to decide whether he was working for himself or for CIE. He was to spread his three intensive work hours over a less intensive eight hour day. Worse still, he was to be transferred to Rosslare Harbour. The decision was made for him. He resigned from CIE on 21 June, 1961.

'I had no qualms about resigning from CIE to go into the ballroom business . . . but I didn't tell my mother until I had actually resigned.'

– 3 –
The Ballroom King

On the afternoon of Thursday, 28 April, 1994, Taoiseach Albert Reynolds visited the Point Depot in Dublin where arrangements were being finalised for the Eurovision Song Contest. This was the country's second time in a row to stage the contest.

'If you win three times, you get to keep it,' quipped Albert Reynolds to RTE's Director General, Joe Barry. Barry shuddered at the thought. But the comment proved prophetic. Forty-eight hours later, against the odds, Ireland had won the contest again, and Joe Barry was facing another £1,500,000 headache.

The atmosphere at the Point Depot was of the kind that Albert Reynolds would have savoured in his old ballroom days. Musicians arriving, testing their instruments, seating being put in place, and everywhere a sense of excitement. The wonders of science and technology had transformed the scene from the days when Albert Reynolds first started to run dances.

Looking back on more than thirty years of history it is difficult to imagine the effect the showband era had on Irish society. The ballrooms of romance fully belonged to the category of a social service. Alcohol free, they stood out like an oasis of glamour and warmth across the country. The good ones were well-lit, well-run and had the best bands. Once and for all, they buried the local dances where stiff-lipped parish priests glared across the dance floor at warm-blooded couples. The ballrooms gave the country a new romance.

Central to the ballrooms were the showbands.

The showband phenomenon was 'invented' in Northern Ireland by the Clipper Carlton. In his excellent book on the era, *Send 'em Home Sweatin'*, Cork author Vincent Power recounts how the Strabane band lit the fuse that led to the showband explosion of the '60s by literally putting a show into their stage routine.

'It was known as *Juke Box Saturday Night*. While orchestras provided the musical accompaniment to the dance floor, the Clippers became the centre of attention. They became entertainers, wore colourful suits, got rid of the music stands and moved around the stage. The Clippers transformed the dancing ritual simply by becoming themselves.'

While the idea of getting rid of the music stands sounds like a very simple idea now, it was a huge, risky step at the time. But it worked. The band drew thousands into any venue they played, north or south of the Border. Their music knew no religious or political differences. The band was as popular in Cork as it was in Belfast. The earnings of the band were huge in comparison with ordinary wages at the time. They were among the first to demand a percentage of the door-takings rather than a straight fee. At 50 per cent of an average crowd of 2,500 at 5/- a head, their fee was £312, the equivalent of about £5,000 in today's terms. By the early '60s some of the Irish showband musicians were among the best paid in the world.

But if the Clippers were the trail-blazers, the kings of the Irish ballrooms were the Royal.

They emerged from an unlikely beginning in Waterford where a few musicians – Michael Coppinger, Charlie Matthews, Jim Conlon and Jerry Cullen – decided to form a band and play together on their free nights. They invited in another local lad, Tom Dunphy, because they knew he could sing and had access to his father's double-bass, and were also joined by Brendan Bowyer, the son of a local publican and classical music teacher, who joined to play the trombone. The band was launched as semi-professional on 22 September, 1957. Soon they were attracting thousands of fans up and down the country.

The Royal began to tour abroad, first in Britain and then further afield in the United States. They were the first Irish band to record a single *Come Down The Mountain Katie Daly* for EMI in 1962. In 1963 they shot to Number One in the Irish charts with *Kiss Me Quick.* More hits followed, notably *The Hucklebuck* in 1965.

On a tour in Liverpool in 1963 they were preceded by a little known support group called 'The Beatles'. The relatively unknown group of four did not have a good night. Afterwards, in the carpark, one of them, Paul McCartney, ate a bag of chips and gazed at the Mercedes wagon belonging to the Royal Showband. Bowyer declined McCartney's offer of a chip, but advised him that if the group stuck together they could do well!

Central to the success of the Royal Showband was their manager, TJ Byrne. A former salesman from Carlow, he soon transformed the band's profile, and with it their earning powers. They reached new dizzy heights of fame. They lived like kings and enjoyed life's luxuries. According to author Vincent Power, the Royal were as important to the young people of Ireland in 1963 as U2 were more than a quarter of a century later.

TJ Byrne also began to demand percentages for the Royal. No serious ballroom owner could afford to ignore the band, even at a ratio of 60/40 in favour of the Royal.

'Often,' says Byrne, now living in Carlow, 'it was difficult even to get a few quid out of some people. So I decided we would go on a percentage basis.'

'He was a great man for marketing the Royal,' Albert Reynolds said of TJ Byrne. 'He introduced a whole lot of marketing skills that weren't apparent in the business.'

Soon more showbands were emerging – Butch Moore and the Capitol, Joe Dolan and the Drifters, Brendan O'Brien and the Dixies, Dickie Rock and the Miami, Eileen Reid and the Cadets, and many others.

With the showbands and their managers there even came a new coded language, adapted from the beng-lang: 'Duke of Kent' was 'rent', 'chicken's neck' a cheque, 'tin of fruit' a suit, and 'jo-maxi' a taxi.

'We used to have conversations in pubs and restaurants that no-one but ourselves could understand,' says Paddy Cole, then sax player with the Capitol. 'The "Spoofer" Jordon, who was our driver, was fluent in the language.'

To the outsider the showband business looked glamorous. But inside, the reality was often very different as the new 'stars' fell victim to alcohol, broken marriages and other problems associated with the fast lane.

'Fair enough, we always stayed in the best hotels and ate the best food,' says Paddy Cole, 'and, of course, we all wore sheepskin coats, the status symbol of the age.'

It was against this background that Albert Reynolds and his brother Jim built their first ballroom in Rooskey.

It was the Brylcreem era and, with RTE television yet to go on air, the local ballroom became the entertainment mecca for whole communities in rural and urban Ireland.

In 1957 Jim Reynolds had returned home from Australia with £5,000 and Albert convinced him to go into partnership in the ballroom business. They bought a site beside their old home in Rooskey, secured a loan from the local branch of the Munster and Leinster Bank, and the Cloudland was born. The name was appropriate for the new era of romance and escapism.

While in Australia Jim Reynolds had worked in the construction industry where he acquired useful skills. He concentrated on the building side of the business, while Albert booked the bands and looked after the money. In building Cloudland the Reynolds brothers concentrated as far as possible on employing local labour.

Paddy Glennon lived a quarter of a mile from Albert Reynolds and he supplied the timber.

Another local man to do well, publican Dessie Hynes, who then ran a wholesale sweet business, got the contract to supply the Cloudland and later ballrooms. That kind of self-reliance, according to Paddy Glennon, was typical of Midland business people.

'Albert came from the same mould,' he said later. 'He started from small beginnings. He wasn't afraid to take off his coat and put his hand to anything. That, and never taking "No" for an answer, is typical of the people in the Midlands.'

There were the cynics, of course.

'Some people said we were mad,' Albert recalled later. 'The ballroom thing was supposed to be a joke. It couldn't be done. Everyone thought we were lunatics to build a ballroom where there was no population. But people travelled forty and fifty miles to the dances if the attraction was big enough.'

In 1959, for example, over 6,000 people attended the Miss Quinnsworth Final in the Cloudland where May Noonan from County Kerry emerged the winner.

Among those who travelled to Rooskey to dances in the Cloudland in those days was Frank Murray from Carrick-on-Shannon. Frank later joined the civil service and was appointed Cabinet Secretary to the Albert Reynolds' Government.

The success of the Cloudland in Rooskey encouraged Albert and Jim Reynolds to expand, and they built another ballroom, the Roseland, in Moate. Albert Reynolds appears to have had no actual stake in either of these ballrooms, but worked closely with his brother in both.

The cash flow from the Cloudland was good. The money from the mineral bar generally paid the staff, and they shared the door takings with the band.

'We used the cash flow from the first ballroom to build the second and so on,' said Albert. 'In fairness, the bank kept running with us. Unless you have a bank to run with you in this type of business, you just can't operate.'

The lifestyle put tremendous pressure on Albert Reynolds, but he survived. Being a teetotaller – although he smoked heavily – helped him to maintain the pace. But he will never forget the first night after his honeymoon in July 1962.

He had been running a Show Dance in Athy and was driving home in his Austin A40 on the road between Edgeworthstown and Longford when he started to nod off. His car collided with a lorry and ended up on its side in the ditch. The night's takings, in a bag thrown loosely in the boot, were scattered everywhere. The smell of whiskey from broken bottles, returned from the Show, filled the air.

Just back from his honeymoon in Majorca, he and his brother Jim had had a heavy day tending the bar. Tiredness had caught up. Albert Reynolds was all right, although he still carries a slight scar, which he sustained in the accident, over his right eye.

In 1961 Jim Reynolds bought the Longford Arms Hotel from the O'Shea family, and Albert moved his office there. Old records in the Companies Office in Dublin Castle show that Albert Reynolds initially owned a 33 per cent stake in it. With the aid of a secretary he ran the day-to-day business of the ballrooms from this base.

In 1961 the brothers also established Reynolds Dancing Ltd, a company in which they each took a 50 per cent stake. But Jim Reynolds continued to own the ballrooms in Rooskey and Moate on his own. Next came Fairyland in Roscommon, Dreamland in Athy, Lakeland in Mullingar, Jetland in Limerick, Barrowland in New Ross, Rockland in Borris-on-Ossory, Borderland in Clones and Moyland in Ballina. At the height of their business, the Reynolds brothers owned fourteen separate ballrooms that stretched from Strabane to Limerick, and rented others.

The formula was always the same. Jim Reynolds was at all times the main player, building ahead in advance, while Albert helped to look after the bands.

'We'd identify the sites on a map first and decide where to go next strategically,' he recalled. 'Building a ballroom took about three and a half months from start to finish. I'd tell Jim to give me a date for completion. Everything had to be finished for the opening night and I would do the rest.'

As the empire expanded, part-time or full-time managers were appointed to run different ballrooms. A former manager with the Clipper Carlton, Maxie Muldoon, was appointed to run the Jetland in Limerick, the biggest ballroom in the chain. Saturday night saw regular crowds of between 3,000 and 4,000 people coming from a huge hinterland of Clare, Limerick and Tipperary to hear one of the big showbands.

Part of the skill of managing the chain of ballrooms was to know what band would attract a large crowd in what area, and which were the good nights in any one particular part of the country. The Melody Aces were a big draw in Rooskey and the Midlands, whereas the Dixies were huge in the South.

The Reynolds brothers used the big bands such as the Royal to open new ballrooms. While Royal manager TJ Byrne says he did most of his business with Jim Reynolds, he recalls Albert always supervising one of the halls on the night.

'He had integrity and honesty,' says TJ, 'I could have trusted him with my life. There was no need to have a man watching on the door. You would always get exactly your share. When he was appointed Taoiseach I said that if he brought the same qualities to that job he would be excellent.'

Significantly, a local Midlands band, Joe Dolan and the Drifters, were to get one of their early breaks from Albert Reynolds. Initially it was supermarket guru Pat Quinn who offered them dates around the country in a beauty contest. The Drifters played as supporting act to the Rhythm Boys from Buncrana.

'It was hard trying to catch his eye,' says Drifters' manager, Seamus Casey, who still operates from Mullingar. 'We played for very little in a marquee in Rooskey beside the Cloudland as support to a British band, the John Barry Seven. You had to get dates with the Reynolds chain. They had a status and owned key ballrooms on the circuit around the country.'

But initially Albert Reynolds refused to give the Drifters any dates.

'We weren't a known band then,' recalled Joe Dolan. 'He wanted somebody who would draw people into the hall. He already had people like Donie Collins, the Clipper Carlton, the Capitol, Brendan Bowyer and, of course, Johnny Flynn. A lot of bands were drawing crowds, and we weren't in that league. It took us a long time before we got a gig from Albert. Don't get me wrong, I like Albert, he's a great guy, but he didn't do us any favours in the beginning . . . He wasn't in business to do anyone a favour. He was in it to make bread.'

But eventually the Drifters got the break and became regular performers in the Reynolds chain. Later they opened the Barrowland in New Ross, Co Wexford.

Joe Dolan also points out that the Reynolds family were the first in the country to offer a hot meal to performing bands. Up to that time, and indeed for long after with other proprietors, the staple menu for the night was tea and ham six nights a week.

'The Reynolds were the first to recognise that musicians were human beings, too,' says Seamus Casey. 'As well as a hot meal there was always a crate of beer left behind the stage for the band members for refreshment. It might seem a simple thing, but it was not the done thing at the time. In many cases you had to specify the requirements of the band, but not with Albert Reynolds.'

Paddy Cole, too, remembers being given hot meals by the Reynolds.

'Up to that time you would be normally given a slice of ham so thin you could read the *Evening Press* through it. But the Reynolds family would bring you to a hotel or a house for a hot meal before you started.'

Cole says that the Reynolds brothers also tried to put some heating into the normally freezing ballrooms.

'Albert was the man we were in touch with regarding dates and money,' recalls country music legend Larry Cunningham from Granard, Co Longford. He and the Mighty Avons got their first major break from the Reynolds brothers when they played relief band to the Clipper Carlton at the opening of the Fairyland ballroom in Roscommon.

'Both brothers were very strict businessmen,' said Larry. 'They did a good job by providing good halls. They paid you well, but you had to do your job for them. They were very strict, hard businessmen. But they were also very fair.'

Another former musician turned promoter, Senator Donie Cassidy, says Albert and Jim Reynolds put a professionalism and expertise into the industry that wasn't there before.

'Before them the venues were small and the facilities were bad, but they saw a gap in the market and built magnificent halls with the best of lighting and other facilities.'

A superstar of the era, Dickie Rock and his band, the Miami, also suffered at the hands of poorly run ballrooms. It was a pleasure, he said, to perform in the chain of 'Land' ballrooms owned by Albert and Jim Reynolds. There were decent changing rooms and the band always got a good meal.

'I look at Albert Reynolds' success in politics and in business,' Dickie told journalist Vincent Power, 'and I can see why he is successful. He was honest and straightforward with the bands and treated us great.'

But Albert Reynolds was no saint, and innovative tactics were employed to entice the young people away from the opposition. When Albert Reynolds moved into McGarry's ballroom in Ballyhaunis, Co Mayo, he came into competition with Monsignor James Horan – he later spearheaded the building of Knock Airport – who then ran a dancehall in Toureen. Very soon the news spread that the devil had been sighted in Monsignor Horan's ballroom in

Toureen. Parents panicked and ordered their offspring to stay away. The finger of suspicion, though never proven, pointed in one direction. Monsignor Horan was not pleased and brought up the episode with Albert Reynolds twenty-five years later when he was trying to secure Government support for the building of Knock Airport from Minister Reynolds.

By a strange coincidence the devil turned up a few months later in the Majestic ballroom in Mallow where Jack O'Rourke was also providing stiff competition to the Reynolds chain.

The main rival chain to the Reynolds brothers was Associated Ballrooms, which was established in 1964. It comprised three of the best known men in the business – Con Hynes, Jack O'Rourke and Donie Collins. Between them they covered more than thirty ballrooms right across the country, among them some of the biggest in the land such as The Talk of the Town, Galway, and the Majestic in Mallow.

In addition there were other independent operators around the country who fitted in where the chains left a gap. These included the Oyster in Dromkeen, Co Limerick, owned by Pakie Hayes; the Golden Vale in Dundrum, Co Tipperary, owned by Austin Crowe; the Redbarn in Youghal and the Stardust in Cork City, owned by the Lucey brothers, Murt and Jerry.

In addition to Irish bands, Albert Reynolds also kept an eye abroad for acts that might go down well in the ballrooms around the country. In the early '60s during a jazz phase he booked Kenny Ball and his band six months in advance for a fee of £35 a night. It was something of a risk at the time. However, by the time the band came to play in Ireland they had a Number 1 hit in the charts with *Midnight In Moscow*. Albert had packed halls every night for ten nights.

The profits he made allowed him to buy his home, Mount Carmel, on the outskirts of Longford Town.

'I have great affection for that song, I bought my house on the proceeds of it,' he told journalist Liam Collins of the *Sunday Independent.*

Mount Carmel was bought from a local customs and excise officer and refurbished in a modern style.

He brought Aker Bilk and Roy Orbison to Ireland. He even once booked the Beatles but could not find a venue big enough to take them, and so had to cancel again. He also booked Jim Reeves, who was notoriously fussy over the piano and facilities provided, but had to cancel when Pope John XXIII died. Reeves waived the contract which was for £650 for two spots.

Chain ballroom owners like Albert Reynolds were in a strong position to entice overseas artists as they could guarantee nationwide tours with full houses all the way. Artists to tour Ireland in the early '60s included Hank Locklin, Chubby Checker, Johnny Cash, Jim Reeves, Adam Faith and Little Richard.

The success of the showbands had huge downstream benefits for the Irish economy. Every band needed transport, commonly known as the 'wagon'. They needed instruments, many changes of clothes, and sound equipment. A huge business was created in publicity, advertising and printing.

Such was the effect of the music industry on the economy that Butch Moore of the Capitol Showband, who represented Ireland in the Eurovision Song Contest in 1965 with *Walking the Streets in the Rain*, declared at the height of his fame: 'It's about time this country, from the Government down, dropped the snobbishness and began to realise that the biggest industry in Ireland at the moment is showbands.'

On the publicity front the most important publication was *Spotlight* magazine. Founded by Murt Lucey of Cork and local journalist John Coughlan of the *Evening Echo*, it was the bible of the showbands. A front cover photograph of a showband on *Spotlight* guaranteed a boost in sales and increased bookings. Ballroom owners like Albert and Jim Reynolds closely monitored its contents for news of upcoming bands or signs of new trends in the industry.

In addition to *Spotlight* there was a lesser publication, the *New Musical Gazette*, which was published by Jimmy Molloy on Lower Main Street, Longford. The NMG concentrated largely on the growing Country 'n' Irish fans. Its contributors included Fr Brian D'Arcy, former *Sunday World* editor Colm McClelland and *Sunday Independent* columnist Sam Smyth. The magazine tended to take a humorous view of the industry and was popular for its cartoons. Local businessman Albert Reynolds was a keen supporter of the publication.

According to Jimmy Molloy, now deceased, Albert Reynolds had a pragmatic instinct for viability, but also an almost reckless generosity to venture his hard-earned capital where others would back off.

It was Albert Reynolds who persuaded Molloy that there was an opening for a more local magazine than *Spotlight.*

'The NMG was started as soon as possible,' Molloy told the *Longford Leader* in February '92. 'I wasn't too pleased with the look of it, but the first reaction was good and I think Albert recognised a trier fairly quickly. He simply loves a trier. If you're a worker, he'll give you a break. And, God knows, he fairly works himself.'

Later Molloy told Reynolds that he needed better printing gear, and his next question was, 'How much do you need?'

'Eventually he did what I didn't expect, he paid £1,500, a large sum in those days, for new works and, as if it wasn't good enough, he put us in new premises,' added Molloy.

'I did the right thing and offered him the kind of share his contribution deserved. He didn't want to hear about it, but eventually took a small stake. In all we had five full-time staff there and sometimes more. Think of the impact of that on the local economy.

'Even more eventually benefited from what was a small business move for Albert. Brian D'Arcy and Ken Stuart, Colm McClelland and Sam Smyth, Jimmy Magee and Pat Billings, Derek Davis and the late Donal Corvin all got breaks from Albert's injection into the NMG.'

– 4 –
The Bacon King

All things must come to an end, and it was no different for the showband era. It's difficult to pin-point exactly when the decline set in, but it was noticeable from the late '60s. The causes were many and varied. The attitude of the showbands themselves played no small part.

Undreamed-of earnings and international acclaim bred a sense of false security. Once a band kept producing new songs to a formula there was no apparent reason why it should not go on forever. Gradually the bands began to take their audiences for granted. They charged more and performed for less time. Top of the range bands were taking 60 per cent of the door-takings but were often on stage for less than two hours. Standards also dropped as a glut of poor quality bands tried to jump on board the gravy train.

'Fellows were coming out from under motor cars and down from trees to become showband managers overnight,' was how one observer put it.

Nobody spotted the trend earlier than Albert Reynolds.

'I always believed it was the showbands that killed the golden goose,' he said. 'They used to play a full five-hour programme. I remember queues in Rooskey and Moate at eight o'clock on a Sunday evening in the middle of a hot summer. The bands pulled back and only played two hours or less. People drifted into the pubs and from that grew cabaret.'

It had been a good business for twelve years, but finally Albert Reynolds felt the customers were being short-changed.

'The big stars used to play from 9.00 pm to 1.00 am or from 9.30 pm to 2.00 am,' he told Deirdre Purcell of the *Sunday Tribune.* 'That sort of development worried me. Here were people paying ten shillings and they were listening to a local band for two or three hours before the stars came. I said it to them – that they'd kill the golden goose – and they did.'

Reynolds warned people like Royal Showband manager TJ Byrne of the trend, but Byrne did not agree. Rather the Carlow man blames the ballroom owners for not upgrading their premises and the Government for charging VAT on admission prices and for refusing to grant drink licences to the ballrooms.

Artist Robert Ballagh, who played bass guitar with the Chessmen, blamed the rise of Country 'n' Western music partly for the decline. For him the lyrics and music had become uninteresting. This kind of music became specialised and eventually saw the rise of new stars like Daniel O'Donnell. New embryonic types of music were emerging as epitomised by one of the most talented groups to appear at this time, Horslips, who merged traditional Irish and rock music in a new and exciting way.

Tastes began to change with the ever-fickle public. New forms of entertainment developed, notably the disco for the younger set and cabaret for the older age group. Generally people found both in their local pub or hotel, and had no further use for the cold, sober ballrooms.

For the ballrooms of romance the dream was over.

'A chapter of Ireland's social history had closed,' wrote Vincent Power. 'The lights dimmed on the ballrooms that are now derelict, demolished or being used as bingo halls, workshops, factories, supermarkets, garages or furniture stores. Most of the great landmarks of the era exist in memory only.'

But Albert Reynolds was never in ballrooms for the music. That was for others. He was there to make money, and had already experimented with alternative forms of entertainment. During the '60s a new game craze – bingo – began to take over Ireland. Never one to let an opportunity pass, Albert Reynolds noted its popularity and was the first in the country to introduce a £1,000 bingo session. It took place in the Roseland in Moate on 15 December, 1963. The punter bought as many books as he or she liked for £1 each, and aimed at a top prize of £1,000. The session brought in £2,200. Together with a young helper, Albert Reynolds sold the tickets at the door, went to the microphone and called the numbers, sold the sweets and minerals at half-time, closed up and went home. Profit for the night – a cool £1,100, the equivalent of around £12,000 in today's figures. Soon the ballroom king had become a bingo king, although not always with the same success.

A session in Mullingar after Christmas suffered badly due to heavy snow, but Albert paid up the £1,000 anyway to everyone's astonishment. He lost £1,000 on the night. This ability to live up to his commitments even though it meant suffering heavy losses was a key ingredient of his successful business career.

In 1966 Albert Reynolds took a decision to get out of the ballroom business, although there were still five or six good years left.

His exit from the ballroom scene was hastened by a serious business difference with his brother Jim. The cause of the dispute is believed to have centred on ownership of some of the ballrooms, and in particular of the Longford Arms Hotel. This distasteful episode saw Albert initiate legal proceedings against his brother, but the issue was settled outside of court for a reputed figure of £50,000. The wound took many years to heal but the brothers are long back on friendly terms.

'It was silly, stupid, and should never have happened,' Joe, the eldest of the family, said later.

'We had a policy difference after the expansion of the ballrooms in the late '60s,' Albert told journalist Michael Hand of the *Sunday*

Tribune. 'We settled out of court, I'm not going to tell you how much for . . . it certainly caused a stand-off in relations but that has since been amended fully.'

It was the wives of the two brothers, Kathleen and Anne, and the children, who effected a reconciliation.

At the time of his departure it is estimated that his ballroom interests extended to a 50 per cent stake in six locations owned by Reynolds Dancing.

In the meantime the brothers had also widened their interests into the property market. In 1964 Albert and Jim established two property companies, JP Reynolds Ltd and Lands Ltd, with Albert holding a 25 per cent stake in each. These companies bought and sold a number of properties, mainly in Co Longford, and are understood to have been quite profitable.

On 26 June, 1966, Albert Reynolds formally resigned from the board of Reynolds Dancing, the Longford Arms Hotel, Lands Ltd and JP Reynolds. At the same time his shares were transferred to Jim's wife, Anne.

Jim Reynolds was to continue on with the ballroom business for some more years, combining this with property and other interests. In recent years he bought the Fountain Blue Bar outside Longford Town. His son, John, runs the popular Dublin night spot, the POD, on Harcourt Street.

Some of Jim's interests have caused his name to turn up in the newspapers occasionally.

In April 1992 he was levied £4,800 under the terms of the *Derelict Sites Act* which had just come into effect. The levy was in relation to numbers 4 and 6 Elgin Road, Ballsbridge, Dublin, which he owns. Both buildings had been in flats but had fallen derelict. In the summer of 1994 Dublin Corporation was in the process of initiating legal proceedings in pursuit of a further levy of £10,680 for the years 1993 and 1994 in relation to the same houses.

In the summer of '94 Jim Reynolds was in dispute with the music copyright organisation, PPI, for a sum of between £140,000 and £167,000 for music played in the Longford Arms Hotel. The PPI were also seeking a sum of between £25,000 and £26,000 from his son John.

The Longford Arms Hotel was back in the headlines in July 1994 when it was included in an area of Longford designated for urban renewal. The Odeon Cinema on Bridge Street, in which the Reynolds family have a 25 per cent stake, was also included. A number of other designated properties were owned by Albert Reynolds' long-time friend, Noel Hanlon. Also included was a section of the meat factory owned by Larry Goodman.

The toilets of the Longford Arms are located in the basement of the Courthouse. The Courthouse had been a source of controversy as to whether or not it should be restored and preserved.

Claiming that the presence of the toilets underneath the Courthouse made it very attractive to the owner of the Longford Arms and less so to anybody else, Progressive Democrat TD Michael McDowell immediately called on the Government to issue a full statement on the nature and extent of urban renewal in Longford.

The Minister for State with responsibility for urban renewal, Emmet Stagg, defended the decision saying it was a 'logical extension' of the area which was previously designated for renewal.

However, he conceded that Longford's Main Street would not in itself have merited designation, but said the backland area behind it was particularly derelict and offered the potential of creating new streets.

'I wouldn't know, and wouldn't need to know who the owners were,' he added.

Out of the ballroom business in 1966, Albert Reynolds found himself with some time on his hands. There was a bit more time for other interests, notably to indulge his passion for racing.

Longford man Dessie Hynes, who later became a well-known Dublin publican, brought him to his first race meeting in Ballybrit.

'Dessie Hynes was the only man in Longford who could get you to Ballybrit in forty-five minutes,' said Albert Reynolds in 1991, 'and he's still alive.'

'We really did spend an awful lot of time in cars, whether it was working for business or for the Fianna Fáil party,' Dessie Hynes recalls. 'I'll always remember the Reynolds' dashboard with several half-empty cigarette boxes swaying across at every sharp bend. I suppose we were all fast drivers. Speed limits were new at the time.'

Albert Reynolds would drop in regularly to Dessie Hynes' shop at 10 Main Street, Longford, for a chat. There, in a backroom, he met a brother-in-law of Dessie's, Neilus Corkery, who devised a betting system with Albert providing the finance. They began with £1. If they lost that on day one, they doubled their bet on day two and so on. They won and lost for several days until Albert finally had to pay out a bet for £256, a sizable sum in those days. Luckily the horse won, and there was a paltry £1 profit. Albert Reynolds made a hasty exit from this novel scheme.

Such sessions of speculative financial planning in Hynes' back room were frequently interrupted by an urgent telephone call from Kathleen Reynolds to tell Albert to bring home the milk and bread at once!

Racing outgoings did not, of course, stop simply at Hynes' shop or Ballybrit Racecourse. The decision to head for Ballybrit could be taken at a moment's notice. A Longford group including Albert Reynolds, Peter Reynolds from Lanesborough, Davy Shearin, Dessie Hynes and others, made annual trips to Cheltenham, Listowel and Ballybunion.

'I don't know how Albert put up with us down at the Field Bar where we'd meet in Ballybunion,' says Dessie. 'He didn't drink and many among us did. There were some great nights in the Field. There were great characters there like the late Smiler Fay and Tommy Noel Donlon who would stay up until all hours in the morning. There was a small Longford community in Ballybunion for the races and Albert wouldn't miss it for the world.'

Those who travelled with him remember Albert for his cool head, particularly on one dreadful plane journey from Leeds-Bradford to London. Dessie Hynes had been to a toy fair, and Albert Reynolds had gone along for the fun of it. When the fair ended, the duo decided to head for London, and boarded a small plane. The plane took a dive and lost 300 feet in a split second, frightening everyone and turning a few stomachs.

'But there was Albert,' Dessie Hynes recalls, 'cool as you like. He is still flying in small planes and helicopters today, something I never did again.'

In those days Albert Reynolds was also a great eater. Everywhere he went he carried a supply of Mars bars with him until the diagnosis of diabetes put an end to it. Such was the addiction of his sweet tooth that in his Longford home he used to keep a tin of McVitie's Victoria cream biscuits under the bed for emergency supply during the night.

'When in Dublin we'd eat in the Ashling on Parkgate Street' says Dessie Hynes. 'You should see him tear through a dinner. He must have been burning energy.'

No stranger to road crashes, Albert, accompanied by Dessie Hynes, one afternoon crashed into a van turning right off the main road to the West on the Dublin side of Moyvalley. When he appeared in court District Justice Dinny O'Donoghue bluntly told the budding Taoiseach: 'Stop pointing your finger at me'. In this instruction Judge O'Donoghue failed dismally.

It wasn't all fun though, and Albert Reynolds along with Dessie Hynes had already begun to show an interest in working for their community.

Later Albert admitted that for a time it was a matter of a toss of a coin as to which of them would run for election.

'Dessie Hynes could be Minister for Finance only for he changed his mind,' Reynolds, then Minister himself, told the Annual Dinner of the Longford Association in 1991 which nominated Hynes as Longford Man of the Year.

In 1965 Reynolds, Hynes and three others, Longford Fianna Fáil TD Frank Carter, engineer Larry Donegan, and Matty Lyons, who was later to become a partner in C&D Petfoods, decided to build the first ever inland swimming pool in the country. It was a brave undertaking at the time. They formed the Longford Development Company and each bought one hundred £1 shares (the cheques were lodged in a safe in Dessie Hynes' shop, but never cashed).

Neil Blaney was Minister for Local Government at the time and the project was to receive a 50 per cent Department grant. Longford County Council was to levy a penny in the pound on rates for its contribution. The local company had to find a balance of between £2,000 and £3,000. The contract to supply and build the pool went to Albert Luykx, who was later to feature in the Arms Trial. He, in turn, sub-contracted the construction work to a Dublin firm, E Kevlighan and Sons.

Deputy Frank Carter was appointed Chairman of the Longford Development Company, Albert Reynolds Vice-Chairman and Dessie Hynes Secretary. The contract price, approved at a board meeting on 23 June, 1965, was for £15,985. The pool was to measure eighty-two feet by twenty-five feet, and to be sited at the Market Square. The 66,000 gallon pool could be heated to seventy-two degrees even at freezing temperatures outside. The water was removed automatically four times an hour, purified, chlorinated, heated and returned to the pool by three vacuum filters. It was amazing technology for the Longford Town of 1966. The Longford Development Company agreed to all the maintenance costs of £5,000 for the first three years of the pool's operation.

The minutes of a board meeting of 6 June, 1966, record that Albert Reynolds 'should act as pool manager for three months from the date of opening'.

The pool was officially opened by Minister Neil Blaney on 28 June 1966 at a colourful function attended by politicians from far and wide.

However, major disagreement erupted on the management of the company and the minutes of the LDC in September 1967 record a discussion 'in a heated manner'.

Deputy Frank Carter told the meeting that with the possible exception of Dessie Hynes, none of the directors devoted sufficient time and interest to the affairs of the company. The minutes continue: 'A Reynolds angrily contested that remark and said he had been engaged almost full-time in the affairs of the company to the neglect of his own affairs, and the other directors agreed with him that Mr Carter's remarks should not apply to him. F Carter refused to acknowledge this, and A Reynolds offered his resignation and attempted to leave but was prevailed on to remain. After some more argument F Carter got up and left, and in his absence A Reynolds as Vice-Chairman assumed the chair.'

Later the meeting passed a resolution appointing Dessie Hynes as managing director of the company with full powers for the next eighteen months.

To raise their part of the finance the Longford Development Company ran carnivals and dances, usually held at the Longford Arms Hotel. Albert Reynolds used his connections with the showbands to book top-class acts at attractive rates. However, the split between himself and his brother Jim caused some showbands to cancel their commitment as they did not want to offend Jim Reynolds.

A dispute with the Drifters ended up in the Circuit Court in Mullingar where the Longford Development Company were awarded £330 for breach of contract. Court proceedings were also threatened with the Mighty Avons, but the band finally agreed to give a free night in lieu of the cancelled performance.

Albert Reynolds disagreed with the attitude of some of his fellow directors and resigned from the company. He later built a private swimming pool in his own house, Mount Carmel. ('It's not true it cost £30,000 – I got it done on direct labour for £3,500.')

The final minutes of the LDC on 17 October 1969 record the handing over of the swimming pool and the maintenance to Longford County Council. Still operating successfully in the town, the pool underwent a £100,000 refurbishment programme in 1991. But the credit for this remarkable initiative to build the country's first inland pool goes to Albert Reynolds and the members of the Longford Development Company.

Meanwhile Albert Reynolds, with money in his pocket, was looking around for a new venture. Matty Lyons, whose family was in the meat business, knew of a bacon factory for sale in the Liberties in Dublin. Patrick Kehoe's, originally Kehoe-Donnellys, was the oldest plant in the capital and was in need of major reinvestment.

'A brother of mine, Denis, was interested in buying Kehoe's, but I advised him against it,' says Matty Lyons. 'He eventually bought a plant in Charleville, Co Cork.'

Albert Reynolds heard of the sale of Patrick Kehoe's.

'I was floating around looking for new opportunities at that time,' he said. 'I was advised to look at a bacon factory, Patrick Kehoe's, on Francis Street. I knew nothing about the business and it was losing a fortune. I went to look at it and the property itself seemed worth the price of £60,000, so I bought.'

Albert Reynolds went into pigs. The office from which he managed the plant was just a few doors down from the Tivoli Theatre. The killing plant was across a side-street on Garden Lane.

He looked after the old women who were natives of the Liberties. For 'a few pounds, a bit of meat' you didn't need any security in return.

'Nobody, but nobody, ever broke into that property,' said Albert. 'I could leave my car open, briefcase, coat, anything in it . . .'

Rita Ryder, who lives on Carman's Hall at the rear of the factory, remembers Albert Reynolds parking his Mercedes on the street outside her door.

'There was no joy-riding then or stealing cars, but we used to keep an eye on it for him anyway,' she says.

Rita was one of Albert Reynolds' first guests on Saturday 6 June 1992, when he officially opened his offices in Government Buildings to the public. A picture of the building, signed by the Taoiseach, hangs in her front hallway.

One story surrounding Albert Reynolds' tenure on Francis Street relates to a time when there was industrial trouble when some producers decided to cut off supplies. The local women came to the rescue. 'You leave us the keys of the factory, Mr Reynolds,' they said to him.

Albert did as required and never asked any questions, but every morning when the pickets arrived promptly at eight o'clock for official opening, they were too late. Mysteriously there were already 150 pigs in the pens.

The women had done their own negotiations with their contacts and every night went out with flashlights to guide the luckless pigs through the narrow streets and into 'Mr Reynolds' factory.

When the strike ended, one innocent supplier remarked to him: 'That must be some size of a holding yard you've got in there.'

According to reports, Albert Reynolds turned the factory round and made it profitable within a year.

The factory was divided into two sections, the killing plant on Garden Lane and the curing hall at nearby Spitalfields. Each evening when the day's killing was finished workers in the factory would load up all the bacon carcasses onto hand carts and wheel them down the street to the hall in Spitalfields.

The day-to-day running of the plant was largely in the hands of two well-known men in the area, Christy Barron and Johnny Guy.

Having taken the entire shareholding of the company himself, Albert Reynolds concentrated on the export end of the market and on raising productivity. He kept employment steady at Kehoe's, except for natural wastage and the business continued successfully until he sold it in 1973. At the time the Department of Agriculture was seeking rationalisation in the industry and Albert Reynolds availed of the scheme by surrendering his bacon export licence.

The factory was damaged by a fire shortly before it closed and it lay idle for a few years.

In 1971 it was rented out on a trial basis by the Coyle Brothers who recommenced killing pigs for the home market.

'Albert said to me how much did it cost to repair the fire damage and he deducted that from the rent,' Harry Coyle recalls. 'We only had a gentleman's agreement but he stuck to his word. When we finally bought the factory in 1973 he had been offered a higher price than us, but he never mentioned the fact. He stuck to the deal.'

Today the factory is still operating successfully with a modern killing line installed. The area was included in the Urban Development Programme announced by Environment Minister Michael Smith in July 1994.

It was during this time that Albert Reynolds began to develop his first political interest. Commuting to his Longford home a few times a week he regularly gave a lift to the local Independent Dáil Deputy, Joe Sheridan, for whom he worked during elections.

While he was in charge of Kehoe's bacon plant he attended the Arms Trial at the Four Courts practically every day.

There, former Minister, Charles Haughey and three others, Captain Kelly, John Kelly (a militant Republican from Belfast) and Albert Luykx (the man who had been involved in the Longford swimming pool) were charged with trying to import arms illegally. The District Court had earlier dismissed charges against another former Minister, Neil Blaney, but the other four were sent for trial to the Special Criminal Court.

The trial opened on 6 October and ended just over two weeks later on 22 October, when all four were found not guilty. The jurors took two hours and twelve minutes to reach their verdict. During his summing up, Mr Justice Seamus Henchy said it was not possible to reconcile the differences in evidence between Charles Haughey and another former Cabinet colleague, Jim Gibbons.

'The simple reason I attended the Arms Trial was because, like everyone else at the time, I was madly interested in the affair,' Albert Reynolds said later. 'And it was handy for me to walk across the Liffey from the factory.'

But Albert Reynolds had still not severed his connection with the music industry. Mindful of the trend in the business and the emergence of cabaret as the new form of entertainment, he and Dessie Hynes travelled around looking at pubs with a view to a joint venture.

Dessie Hynes located a venue in Malahide and paid a £1,000 deposit. However, they failed to raise the balance in various banks. Then, in an unexpected move, Reynolds suddenly raised the money in the Bank of Ireland himself and bought the pub in his own name. Hynes eventually got his deposit back.

The property was owned by Mrs Neilon Walsh and she ran it as a small hotel. A local Garda was a semi-permanent resident. Albert bought the premises for £33,000 and converted it into an impressive cabaret centre called 'The Showboat'. Ahead of its time, the Showboat had a capacity for over 1,000 people.

Jimmy Molloy, publisher of the *National Musical Gazette* remembered Albert in those days:

'I used to go to the Showboat with him and saw him get behind the bar and serve like the hammers all night, then back into the car and home again.'

There was some difficulty, however, with the licence later. But the Showboat burned to the ground on a very windy night in the summer of 1970. It is understood to have been insured for a figure of £83,800. Later Reynolds told *Business and Finance* magazine that the place was 'definitely underinsured'.

The site was later sold off for a shopping centre.

Albert Reynolds sold the bacon-curing plant and returned to Longford. Around this time he became involved in his most colourful enterprise of all, fish exporting.

Firstly, he set up a salmon exporting business, acting on a tip that the variety would be scarce. The salmon were provided by the fishermen in Donegal – in one season he bought the entire catch from Burtonport.

But Albert Reynolds was an outsider in the fish-exporting business and he consequently found great difficulty in securing supplies.

'All the fishing cartels ganged up on me, Billingsgate market ganged,' he said. Suddenly he was stuck with £100,000 of unmarketable fish. He held his nerve, and his frozen fish, until the following Christmas when he was able to sell it for smoking. 'I got out of it OK. . . .'

The experiment with grand live lobster and crayfish was not as successful.

Albert contracted to supply fresh lobsters and crayfish to the French and Spanish markets, but was hampered by an air strike. He solved the problem by buying and converting an executive de Havilland jet.

To fly the plane he hired a large, colourful, Caribbean pilot named Captain Charles. Captain Charles had been meddling in the meat business around the world for some time and had key business contacts.

Everything was organised to run like clockwork. Captain Charles was to collect the fish, fly it direct to the markets, collect the money and return for the next load. But there weren't enough fish to fill the contracts. In desperation Albert went to England to buy the fish.

'The fish venture was not one of my most practical experiments,' he remarked later. Albert Reynolds got out of the fish business.

'I decided I'd had enough and gave the plane to the pilot. There were enough engine hours on it anyway,' he said.

Captain Charles ended up for a time in prison in Scotland – although this had nothing to do with his salmon exporting exploits – and the jet was impounded.

During these risky adventures Albert Reynolds admitted that he often sailed close to the wind, and indeed lost money in the fish export business. But he added: 'I got a fine cocktail cabinet from the executive jet'.

In 1973 Albert Reynolds started ABC Finance, a hire-purchase company based in Longford. The other shareholders were two local businessmen, Brian Nerney and Charlie Lee. The company was involved in the hire-purchase of cars and machinery.

However, it never developed very successfully.

'ABC was never seen as anything more than a local finance company serving a local need. We're still continuing to do this with the resources available to us,' he told the *Longford Leader* in the run-up to the '77 general election.

'It went quite well early on, but then it was neglected,' Charlie Lee told *Business and Finance* magazine. 'It was certainly not Albert's fault. He did a lot to keep it going but it was gradually wound down.' ABC was eventually sold off to a car dealer who dissolved it entirely some years later.

In yet another venture in 1974, Albert Reynolds established AR Trading, understood to stand for Albert Reynolds Trading. This company had a registered office at a solicitor's premises in Longford Town. The exact purpose of the company is not entirely clear, although the following year it acquired a property on Dublin Street, Longford. It was later used, apparently, by Albert Reynolds to acquire the *Longford News*.

To these interests was added a share in the Odeon Cinema in Longford. Albert Reynolds, complete with white Mercedes, had arrived in style.

He was now a leading entrepreneur, relying on his gut instinct.

'To be a risk-taker, to go after opportunity, I often heard it said that if you're too well educated, you'll overanalyse the risk and you won't take it,' he said. But all the time he operated on one underlying principle – you never personally underwrite anything.

'Banks are in the business of selling money, in the business of making decisions. Why should I put everything, my house and my family on the line for them?' he asked.

– 5 –
The Petfood King

July 3, 1984. A large St Bernard dog stood poised outside the Irish Goods Council Headquarters in Sandymount, Dublin. Soon the Minister for Industry and Trade, John Bruton, arrived and was separated from a former Minister, Albert Reynolds, only by the large St Bernard who looked determined to keep the peace between the politicians.

Minister Bruton had arrived to launch a new petfood product *Max* on the Irish market.

In his speech, Mr Bruton referred to a new gourmet restaurant in France which served dogs only and offered full waiter service, pre-dinner aperitifs and three course meals on real china. The Minister said he doubted very much whether such a restaurant would do well in Ireland, although he pointed out that the market for canned dog foods at the time in the country was £7,000,000 a year and growing. However, the market was dominated by imported brands which accounted for over 70 per cent of sales. Mr Reynolds' *Max* was the first premium Irish dog food on the market.

'Dogs everywhere love it,' boasted a proud Albert Reynolds. 'We send it to Italy, to Denmark, all over Europe, and we have never yet had a complaint.'

The notion of the potential for petfood first struck Albert Reynolds while he was running Patrick Kehoe's bacon factory in Dublin.

'I used to pay fellas to take away the offal from the yard. One day they came looking for more money to take the stuff away and I asked, "What are you doing with it anyway?"'

To his surprise he discovered the buyers were freezing it and sending it to England to be made into petfood. And Ireland was reimporting it again.

A few people in the meat business had already tried their hand at petfood, then in its infancy. O'Keeffe's, in the Liberties in Dublin, had a small sideline operation with a brand called *Spot.* This company was later sold to International Meat Packers run by Frank Quinn, and there was a similar small plant in Limerick.

'When I started to build a factory in Longford for cat and dog food people thought I'd gone around the bend,' said Reynolds. 'Nobody buys food for cats and dogs they told me. You feed them on scraps off the table.'

Superquinn boss, Senator Fergal Quinn, remembers the pick-up in the petfood market in the early 1960s.

'Albert Reynolds clearly identified a change in the marketplace,' he says. 'He noticed that people were willing to spend money on petfood rather than simply feed their animals scraps from the table. The timing was critical. If he had been five or six year earlier he would have been too soon, and if he had been five or six years later, he would probably have missed the boat.'

The C&D petfood plant was not, in fact, Albert Reynolds' initial idea at all, but rather that of Longford meat man, Matty Lyons.

Lyons, a member of a well-known family which had extensive interests in the meat industry, had long had a desire to run his own business independently of the family, and identified an opportunity in petfood.

Matty's father, Matt Lyons Senior, had opened an abattoir in Dromod. A second factory was later opened in Longford.

Later still, another brother, Willie Lyons, bought a factory in Charleville which was sold on, first to the Horgan family, then to Halal, and is today owned by the giant Dairygold Group.

Matty Lyons put the plan to Albert Reynolds as they chatted in his red Peugeot 404 one night in Longford Town. Dublin publican Dessie Hynes was in the back seat.

Matty had discussed the idea for some time with a Scottish businessman, John Hammond, who bought the offal from the Lyons factories in Longford and Dromod.

The market looked good. Figures available at the time showed that Britain alone bought £240,000,000 worth of petfood per annum. The plan was to start a modest canning operation, producing 150,000 cases of petfood per year.

A Dublin businessman, Arthur McManus of Foxrock, who had good business connections, and John McShane of Portadown, Co Armagh, were in for 10 per cent each. McShane was, at the time, a director of Robert Wilson's, a meat canning company, and therefore had vital experience. He was also a director of Jessfoods Ltd, a petfood company, owned by Tom McLauchlin from Dublin, who had a factory in Portadown.

Matty Lyons was the major shareholder in the new company, Canine Foods, holding 51 per cent, while Albert Reynolds took the remaining 29 per cent.

Documents lodged with the Companies Office in Dublin Castle show that Canine Foods was incorporated on 5 March 1968. Matty Lyons was registered as the owner of 25,000 shares, Albert Reynolds 12,750 shares and Arthur McManus and John McShane with 2,500 shares each.

But first Canine Foods had to acquire a site.

Matty Lyons' original plan was to site the plant in Longford, but there were numerous objections. Then, one day while on his way to Sligo, he stopped for lunch in a restaurant where he met Frank McGarry from Edgeworthstown. McGarry was a member of the Edgeworthstown Development Association and told Lyons about a field that could be bought outside the town. Lyons lost no time, and went and purchased the five acre site – the current location of C&D Foods – for £600.

The original factory, which was basic but had a laboratory – as much for show to impress the buyers as anything else – was built by local man Hugh Connolly. Much of the equipment was second-hand, which Matty Lyons leased through contacts in the meat industry, although new ovens (retorts) were imported from Britain.

The stream which flowed by the side of the site was insufficient for the plant's needs, but Albert Reynolds, who appeared to have some knowledge of the local water table, arranged for the sinking of two wells on the site.

Environment guidelines were few or non-existent at the time, and there was no effluent treatment plant other than a large sump into which was dumped the blood and other left-overs.

'We had the best-fed magpies in the country,' laughs Matty Lyons, looking back at that time.

But it was a relatively clean industry as the factory mainly processed animal lungs and condemned livers. Lyons of Longford were the main suppliers of offal along with their factory in Dromod, and Hanleys of Rooskey.

None of the investors, says Lyons, put any of their own money into the project which was initially funded by a £50,000 charge on the company and a grant of £45,000 from the IDA.

'Two separate quotations were obtained from the builder, Hugh Connolly,' says Matty Lyons, 'one for the IDA and a lesser real figure for the job.'

Documents filed with the Companies Office on 21 June 1968 show a charge on the assets from the Munster and Leinster Bank, South Mall, Cork, for the sum of £25,000, while further documents filed in October 1969 show a further charge of £22,000 by the Industrial Credit Corporation in Dublin.

The early days were hampered also because of numerous difficulties – including a bank and a cement strike – but the plant was finally completed in 1970. It began operations with a staff of five.

The opening of the plant was officially marked at a reception in Dublin on 1 July 1971. The reception heard a claim that only offal from animals killed in the most humane manner was used by C&D. In order to draw attention to the work being done by the Dublin Society for the Prevention of Cruelty to Animals, the reception was held at the Cats' and Dogs' Home on Grand Canal Quay. It was attended by a number of well-known personalities who sympathised with the aims of DSPCA, including actress Clare Mullen, who was pictured with Albert Reynolds and Matty Lyons in the following edition of the *Longford News*.

At a special meeting in November 1970 they changed the name of the company from Canine Foods Ltd to C&D Pet Foods Ltd when Canine Foods (Britain) Ltd threatened to issue legal proceedings. (This was subsequently changed to C&D Foods Ltd in December 1980.)

There were initial teething problems and difficulties in securing customers. A production manager from a vegetable canning factory had been appointed, but much of the product was unsuitable.

'The British buyers did not want to hear of us,' says Matty Lyons. 'It was a closed operation and very hard to break into. We also had problems in getting the product-mix right, and there were various trials and errors. The most expensive part of the production was the cans and labels. The mix itself cost a pittance.'

Help came in the form of British marketing executive, Norman Spence. Matty Lyons had heard of him through his brother-in-law Brendan Flynn.

'I got a call from Brendan who told me about these two chaps who had a petfood factory and didn't know what to do with it,' says Norman Spence, now living in Wales. 'He wanted to know would I go and see them.'

Spence flew to Dublin where he had an initial meeting with Matty Lyons and the two agreed to do business.

A few weeks later, in November 1970, Spence received a telegram from Lyons saying that Córas Tráchtála had arranged a number of appointments with major buyers in the UK, and asked Spence if he would meet Matty and Albert at Heathrow Airport. Spence met them as arranged and took them on their round of calls where he knew the buyers.

During the week in London, Spence booked theatre tickets for Matty, Albert, and Kathleen Reynolds – who had come over 'to do the shops' – to see *Hair*, which at the time was considered a very daring show.

'While Albert was daring enough to see *Hair*, I found he wasn't very daring when it came to food,' Spence recalls. He later considered it quite a triumph when he managed to persuade Albert to eat a Chinese meal.

Following that week, after a number of meetings and discussions, Spence proposed that he would give Lyons and Reynolds 5 per cent each in his company, Strathmead Marketing Co Ltd, which ran a small van sales operation selling petfood and imported wines to supermarkets, off-licences and Harrods.

In return Spence would become responsible for the development of C&D's total business. He and fellow Strathmead director, Thomas Woolcock, would become directors of C&D, would be paid 25 per cent of the company's profits as well as receiving 10 per cent of C&D's shares. Spence suggested this so that C&D was safeguarded, and he would be paid only when he had developed the business and the company was profitable.

The shares in Strathmead were transferred to Matty Lyons and Albert Reynolds, and Norman Spence, along with Thomas Woolcock and Rathdowney electrician, Alec McKeague, were appointed directors of C&D on 11 February 1971. (John McShane retired as his shares had been bought out by Albert Reynolds without the knowledge of Matty Lyons.)

No C&D shares were transferred to Spence as the company had lost a lot of money.

It was agreed, however, that Spence should receive a small monthly drawing allowance of £160 against future earnings. This continued until May 1974 when Lyons suggested, and Reynolds agreed, that Spence should be paid a reasonable salary plus 10 per cent of the profits and that he should, in due course, receive the 10 per cent of the company's shares due to him.

Lyons also proposed, and Reynolds agreed, that the mortgage on Spence's house should be paid off by C&D. Spence again agreed to this, but no shares were issued, nor was his mortgage ever paid off.

When Spence came on the scene neither Matty Lyons nor Albert Reynolds knew what to make, how to make it, or if they did produce anything, how they were going to sell it. John McShane, the only one with canning experience, had disappeared from the scene, and the production manager with experience of canning vegetables was now running the factory. He had produced 15,000 cases of dog food which were totally unsatisfactory for the market, and which eventually had to be 'jobbed' off, i.e. sold off at a very low price.

'At the time when I arrived, Albert Reynolds had printed labels with the name "Popeye",' says Spence. 'I told him he could not use this as it was copyright with Disney and would cost a great deal of money. He had not thought of this. I checked the cost of using the name but it was prohibitive.'

Spence set about sorting out the basic problems at the factory before beginning an effective marketing campaign. He started by bringing in a new manager, Bill Murchison, on a consultancy basis to develop appropriate products. At first, things went reasonably well with sales starting to grow. Albright & Wilson asked if they could market C&D's products in Ireland.

But, unfortunately, things soon went badly wrong. Faulty cans were supplied to the factory and there were also some problems with the production line.

'Cans were exploding on the shelves of British supermarkets and you can imagine the problems that caused for an Irish product,' says Spence. 'People weren't sure whether I was working for C&D or for the IRA.'

The problem meant that the attempt to market C&D's products in Ireland failed. Spence says he was not too concerned, however, because the home market was small and it was not a central part of his plan to develop the company in Ireland, but to aim at the Own Label markets in the UK and Europe, with specific potential customers targeted.

Murchison left and the operation began to lose serious money. One evening Matty Lyons had gone to the races in Wexford and later ended up at a house party in Waterford. Late that night there was a telephone call from Albert Reynolds.

'Hello Matty,' said an alarmed Albert, 'I've been trying to find you all day. Do you know how much money the factory has lost in two years? £50,000.'

Matty Lyons paused for a moment. 'Well Albert,' he replied, 'you know you can't lose what you haven't got!'

With Murchison gone, a replacement had to be found and Norman Spence brought in a new man, Mervyn Mudd, whom Matty and Albert appointed as General Manager, promising him 5 per cent of the company's shares.

Mervyn Mudd had spent many years working in research and development in human foods, but had latterly worked in the petfood industry. Spence was particularly keen to engage him because of his background and experience and because, he says, Mudd was a genius at product formulation and development.

Not only that, but he was also a practical, hands-on manager in the factory.

'Mind you,' says Spence, 'it was just as well that he was a practical man because Albert would do everything he could to avoid spending money, and Mervyn was forced to do his product research and development work using a bucket and a hand-mixer, because Albert wouldn't spend a few pounds to buy the proper equipment.'

By 1972 the auditors advised putting the company into liquidation. But the directors continued to press on.

'I told Albert and Matty that they would need strong nerves, but I would make the company successful,' says Spence.

Some respite was achieved when Spence persuaded the IDA to pay the balance of approximately half the grant they had originally agreed to give C&D, but which they had refused to pay.

When Spence asked the IDA why they were not paying up, they said it could not succeed, and had never had a chance of succeeding.

But why, then, had they given part of the grant in the first place? Because, they replied, it had created jobs building the factory, and it would eventually be useful to someone.

'Without Norman Spence and Mervy Mudd the place would not have taken off,' says Matty Lyons.

Sales were developed by Spence in Britain and Italy until the major breakthrough came when he managed to secure a contract to supply Sainsbury's with one of their Own Label petfoods.

Sainsbury's was Spence's prime target because of their reputation for demanding the toughest possible standards from their suppliers. Furthermore, becoming a Sainsbury supplier would open the door to other potential customers.

From 3 March 1971, when he made his first call, Norman Spence called every month until 30 November 1973, when the Sainsbury petfood buyer and the technical inspector visited the factory.

Before the visit though, a refurbished filling machine from England had to be installed. The only way it could be delivered in time was for Spence to hire a van and take it over himself. As the machine was very high, he had to hire a furniture van. However, unused to such a vehicle, Spence forgot about its height and demolished part of the balcony of a hotel in which he stayed overnight, but managed to keep the precious machine intact.

When Spence and the Sainsbury men entered the factory in Edgeworthstown, the smell of fresh paint almost knocked them over. Mervyn Mudd and everyone in the factory had been up all night painting, finishing only at 5.00 am in the morning.

After an exhaustive inspection of the factory where nothing was missed, including the staff restroom and toilets, the technical inspector announced that, subject to certain works being carried out and subsequent satisfactory reinspection, the buyer had his approval to go ahead if he wished. The buyer confirmed his wish to C&D, subject to meeting certain other conditions and subject to his director's confirmation.

'When we left the factory to head for Dublin and the flight back to England we heard a huge cheer as we passed through the factory gates. I gathered later that as soon as we had left everyone went down to the pub to celebrate.

'We had partaken the night before, perhaps a little too liberally, of the dark brown holy water of Ireland, and one of the passengers sitting in the back of the car coughed as I drove along, and was then violently sick. Unfortunately, I was directly in his line of fire, and I had another reason never to forget that particular visit. But it was all in the line of duty.'

At that time British companies had suffered unfortunate experiences with Irish manufacturers, and Sainsbury's were unwilling to do business unless they could be reassured. At the end of further questioning, and having been given a guarantee that the factory would be managed by Mudd and the marketing by Spence, a deal was agreed. This deal gave C&D an outlet for an extra 200,000 cases per year initially, with more to come as the business developed. Spence's marketing strategy was to sell high quality products at competitive prices, not poor quality products at low prices, nor even slightly better quality products at the lowest prices.

His prices to Sainsbury's were slightly below those of Sainsbury's other major Own Label supplier, Spillers, but significantly higher than the other smaller manufacturers who were trying to get in, and were at a level that would produce handsome profits if the level of sales was right.

The profits could be seen from the fact that Albert Reynolds received a £90,000 dividend for the years 1974-1976, and that Arthur McManus and Matty Lyons were paid off.

Superquinn chief Fergal Quinn says the strategy to concentrate on one major customer was clever as it avoided the very heavy costs of advertising brands and all that entailed. The success of C&D could be seen from the fact that the efforts of half a dozen others who tried to get into the industry failed dismally.

In 1975 the business took a leap when Sainsbury's ordered a promotion. Spence himself flew to Ireland to join in the round-the-clock shifts that were needed to get out the extra cases. Four weeks later he suffered a heart attack. Before he had fully recovered, his wife, Olive, fractured her skull and spent three weeks in hospital. But she left hospital early to allow her husband to go on an export trip organised by Córas Tráchtála, in which he visited Holland, Sweden and Denmark. This led to the securing of another major customer in Denmark.

But his heart attack in 1975 had an amusing sequel in 1977 when Spence had an insurance medical in Dublin.

Prior to the examination, the Company Secretary, Bob Cumbers, said: 'Norman, for God's sake, don't tell the doctor you have had a heart attack, just say you had a bit of a blast.'

Spence did in fact tell the doctor the truth.

'Jaysus, we can't put that down,' replied the doctor. 'We'll say you went into hospital suffering from exhaustion.'

By now Albert Reynolds, who had been talking to the IDA and the ICC, had his own plans for the company.

Matty Lyons had effectively withdrawn from the day-to-day running of the business and opened a pub in Celbridge, Co Kildare. The then C&D accountant, Bob Cumbers, contacted Matty Lyons and told him that money was being withdrawn from the company, the purposes of which were unclear.

'I came down to the factory unexpectedly one morning and looked at the files but I was not qualified to scrutinise them,' Lyons recalls.

Looking back on the incident Bob Cumbers cannot remember the exact details, but says he would have drawn the matter to the attention of the directors as the accounts had to be certified.

'As far as I was aware the matter must have been sorted out between the parties because nobody ever pursued it with me again,' says Cumbers.

According to Norman Spence, Albert Reynolds told him that the Company Secretary, Bob Cumbers, had seen a letter, and had managed to obtain a copy, confirming that MJ Lyons of Longford had applied to the Department of Agriculture to can intervention beef. MJ Lyons would be supplied with all the materials, beef, cans, and other essentials free, as well as being paid 17p per can for packing and processing. The processing would be carried out at C&D. The operation would last three-four months and, if it were successful, it would mean that the petfood business, so painfully and patiently built up, would disappear.

Spence expressed disbelief but Albert Reynolds insisted it was true, saying the Lyons family would make so much money from the deal they didn't care about C&D, and that Matty had to agree as he owed a lot of money to the family.

Reynolds persuaded Spence, Mudd and Arthur McManus that steps needed to be taken to stop Matty Lyons who was the major shareholder.

He proposed that a directors' meeting and a shareholders' meeting be called and that Spence and Mudd be given the shares they were due. This would reduce every existing shareholder's percentage holding of shares and, most significantly, would reduce Matty Lyons' holding below 50 per cent.

Bob Cumbers cannot recall seeing any such letter, but was aware of pressure being put on Matty Lyons to allow the plant to can intervention beef. No letter was ever produced by Albert Reynolds in the subsequent High Court case.

The directors and shareholders meetings were held on 11 November, 1974, and Matty Lyons met Spence at Dublin Airport to take him to the meetings at the factory.

'I tackled Matty about this and he confirmed that while he did owe money to his family, there was no intention to can beef and no letter applying to do so,' says Spence. 'Matty said Albert was trying to get rid of him for other reasons.'

'I knew there were problems about cash that was held in the office, but I never saw the books because Bob Cumbers, the Company Secretary, had been given strict instructions by Albert that I was not to see them under any circumstances. I did manage to see salary payment details several years later though, and discovered that Kathleen Reynolds was being paid £3,000 nett/month.'

The directors' meeting was duly held on 11 November 1974, when two resolutions were passed to be recommended to the shareholders. These resolutions were to issue Spence's and Mudd's shares and to increase the company's share capital. Matty Lyons opposed both resolutions saying they should be deferred until the company's AGM was held. Albert Reynolds argued that as both Spence and Mudd were present, there should be no further delay in issuing the shares that were due to them. The resolutions were passed on a show of hands.

There then followed an EGM of the three existing shareholders, Lyons, Reynolds and McManus.

Reynolds took the meeting as chairman, and proceeded to read the first resolution.

Before he had finished, he was interrupted by Lyons who demanded a vote, but Reynolds ignored him. Again Lyons interrupted, repeating his request for a vote. Reynolds replied saying he could have a vote when he had completed reading the resolution. When he had finished he asked for those in favour to show by raising their hands. He and Arthur McManus did so. Then he asked for those against to show. Matty Lyons raised his hand.

'Two in favour, one against – resolution carried,' declared Reynolds.

'You can't do that,' shouted Matty Lyons. 'I have more shares than you.'

At this point the company's auditor, Bernard Carroll, interrupted to say it was a poll Matty Lyons wanted.

'Yes,' replied Matty, 'it's a poll I wanted.'

'Too late,' said Albert, 'the resolution has been passed, and can't be reopened.'

Matty Lyons refused to take any further part in the discussions and actions that followed. Spence and Mudd were allocated their shares, Spence paying £1,500 for his, which was to be repaid to him by way of a future bonus. The members voted him an immediate bonus to pay the balance.

Mervyn Mudd was similarly voted a bonus, and the Company Secretary was instructed to register their shares immediately.

Matty Lyons was replaced as Managing Director by Albert Reynolds. Lyons reacted swiftly, however, and served a High Court injunction within days. His solicitor, Tom Gannon, was killed some time later when his small aircraft crashed into the Galtee Mountains in Tipperary.

Lyons, no longer a majority shareholder, took his action under the section of the *Companies Act* which protects the rights of minority shareholders, claiming that the directors had acted 'in a manner oppressive to him and in disregard of his interest'.

The case was heard in the High Court, Dublin, on 11 and 12 February 1975 by Mr Justice Kenny, who found in Lyons' favour. The judge ruled that although Reynolds was technically correct in declaring that the resolution had been passed and the matter could not be reopened, Reynolds knew perfectly well that Lyons wanted a vote based on the number of shares held, i.e. a poll.

The result meant that Norman Spence had lost out yet again. As a result of the judge's ruling, the issuing of shares to both him and Mervyn Mudd was also null and void.

'Although,' added Mr Justice Kenny, 'there is no doubt that the shares are due to Spence and Mudd.'

The case created legal precedent in Ireland because that particular section of the *Companies Act* empowered the judge to order one party to sell his/her shares to another, and he ordered Matty Lyons to sell his shares to Albert Reynolds.

It took over two years for the matter to be resolved. In evaluating the worth of C&D the names of three accountancy firms were put forward. Both sides agreed that Owens Murray & Co undertake the study. This eventually saw Matty Lyons receive a pay-off of £44,000.

Lyons formally retired from the board of C&D on 20 May 1977 and his shareholding was transferred to Albert Reynolds.

Matty Lyons bid farewell to C&D, and for a while made plans to build a canning plant producing meat for human consumption. However, these came to nothing. He returned to doing consultative work for the Lyons' factory in Longford Town.

During 1976 there was a minor fire at C&D Pet Foods. A cold store was badly damaged, but had been fully insured.

The autumn of '77 saw a number of other changes at C&D.

Electrician Alec McKeague retired from the board on 22 November as did Arthur McManus. His 2,500 shares were bought out and transferred to Kathleen Reynolds who joined the board of directors also on 22 November. Norman Spence claims neither he nor the other UK director, Thomas Woolcock, were ever notified of this meeting.

When Albert Reynolds finally received Matty Lyons' shares, he asked Norman Spence what he wanted to do with the company.

'He asked me if my children would be interested in going into the business. I said my children would not, but that we should build up the business and perhaps sell it in five to ten years' time unless his children wanted to become involved.'

During this discussion Spence suggested a profit-sharing scheme for all the employees.

'Albert blew up and asked me if I was "fecking crazy"? He said "We don't give those hoors a penny more than we have to." '

This was not the only point of disagreement between Albert Reynolds and Norman Spence.

'We had a major disagreement when the Punt was separated from Sterling. Albert wanted me to sell in Punts because, he claimed, the Punt would rocket against Sterling. I could not convince him that we should sell in Sterling, so I stopped arguing and went ahead and did my own thing – I sold in Sterling. Albert has since boasted of getting a price increase every time the Punt fell due to his "brilliant decision"!'

There was also disagreement between Spence and Reynolds over management styles. On one occasion when Spence was at the factory Reynolds publicly countermanded an instruction that had been given by Mervyn Mudd.

'Two shifts were being worked and Mervyn had asked the staff which times they would prefer to work,' says Spence. 'As this would have no bearing whatsoever on the running of the business, or its profitability, it struck me as a very reasonable thing to do, but Albert thought otherwise.

'When I took him to task for countermanding Mervyn's action, he replied: "You should never give those hoors or factory workers any say in anything." I told him that the more you gave the workers an opportunity to express their views, or participate in decisions which affected them without adversely affecting the running of the factory, the better. Secondly, under no circumstances should he have publicly countermanded Mervyn's action and undermined his authority. But Albert would have none of it – "You tell the hoors what to do and that's that." We agreed to differ.'

C&D continued to grow, but there were strains on capacity, and the company lost its first customer, Dempsters in Liverpool, due to inability to supply in October, 1977. In 1978 further strains appeared when Spence was asked by Sainsbury's in June 1978 to bring over Albert Reynolds because there were serious shortfalls in deliveries.

'We were given an ultimatum – increase production or they would find another supplier,' says Spence.

In December 1979 Albert Reynolds was appointed Minister for Posts and Telegraphs and retired from the board of C&D. He was replaced by Longford solicitor Patrick Groarke who was also listed as a director of ABC Finance and the *Longford News*.

But Albert Reynolds appears to have kept himself fully informed of developments at C&D while a Minister. A telex to Norman Spence from the acting Managing Director of C&D, Peter O'Hara, dated 13 April 1981 stated that 'Albert has been fully informed' (about a shipment) and 'he is in full possession of all the facts as usual'.

Spence recalls that the quality control manager from Sainsbury's was not impressed when he arrived at the C&D plant in May 1980 to find a black flag at half-mast mourning the death of IRA hunger striker, Bobby Sands, in a British jail.

Problems continued right into the 1980s. For example, between 11 June 1982 and 21 April 1983 there were nineteen separate complaints from Sainsbury's.

The situation got so bad at various times that C&D approached two Irish companies, Rex Petfoods and Petpack Ltd, to see if they would produce for C&D, and Norman Spence travelled to Holland to negotiate with a Dutch manufacturer to produce for them. However, none of these companies was able to supply the particular products that C&D needed, and the company staggered on.

In January 1983, C&D paid Sainsbury's £30,000 for loss of profits and the cost of withdrawing stocks from branches.

There were further problems after Bob Cumbers, the Company Secretary, left and was replaced by Michael Difley, who was eventually to become Managing Director.

Meanwhile, in the wake of the Lyons' court judgement, Norman Spence again set about trying to secure his shares and monies. On 23 February, 1979 Albert Reynolds finally signed an agreement with Spence. However, the agreement did not cover the issue of the shares owed to Spence because Reynolds argued that the issue was between himself and Spence and not the company and Spence. But he claimed he had Reynolds' word that he would get the shares.

There was also the evidence of the Minutes of 11 November 1974 and Mr Justice Kenny's statement that there was no doubt but that Norman Spence and Mervyn Mudd were due their shares. Eventually there were to be sworn affidavits from Matty Lyons, Thomas Woolcock and Arthur McManus confirming that 10 per cent of C&D's shares were to be given to him.

In the summer of 1982 Spence finally initiated legal action against C&D for his shares.

A lot of correspondence was exchanged between both sides, although Albert Reynolds as Taoiseach claimed on 30 May 1994 that he 'had not been involved in any way in the running of the company for up to fourteen years'. (In his evidence to the Beef Tribunal, Albert Reynolds said he came back to government in 1987 'having spent four years in opposition, having spent four years developing my own business, which is very allied to this business that we are talking about . . .' (*Tribunal Report*, Chapter 6, page 206/207.)

In a speech in Portlaoise in June 1994 the now Taoiseach said he had 'as required an arm's length relationship with that company (C&D), since I took up ministerial office, so I cannot be accountable for and have no knowledge of its day-to-day business'.

On 28 June 1982, while Minister for Industry and Commerce, Albert Reynolds, however, wrote to Spence telling him he had 'not produced the sales needed'.

In a detailed letter he pointed out that capacity would increase two or three fold when a new factory – to be grant-aided by the IDA – was completed.

He added that it was necessary to introduce a new management structure reporting to Michael Difley, and to set budgets and targets for all management.

'. . . I must point out,' he said, 'that there was never any mention or question of your being paid 10 per cent of the profits, or receiving 10 per cent of the proceeds of the sale if I sell the company.'

(During the 1983/87 Coalition, Taoiseach Dr Garret FitzGerald replaced a Junior Minister, Eddie Collins, when it was revealed that he had attended the board meeting of a family company from which he had resigned on his appointment to office. Collins was present at such a meeting when an application for assistance to a State financial institution was discussed.)

On 12 July 1982 Albert Reynolds, as Industry Minister, publicly rejected reports in a British retail magazine *The Grocer* that two giant British supermarket chains, Sainsbury's and Tesco, were pulling out of deals with C&D because of Ireland's stand during the Falklands crisis. Later Reynolds personally telephoned a Mr Hatch at Sainsbury's on 16 July to reassure him.

On 28 August Minister Reynolds attended a meeting at C&D along with the company's auditor Bernard Carroll, P Gillen, head of Kinnear Consultants, and Patrick Groarke, C&D's solicitor.

Article 26 of Government Procedure Instructions states that 'in so far as business interests to membership of other organisations are concerned, the underlying principle is that no Minister or Minister of State should engage in any activities that could reasonably be regarded as interfering, or being incompatible, with the full and proper discharge by him of the duties of his office'.

On 27 April 1983 Albert Reynolds was again asked by Sainsbury's to come to London to discuss ongoing difficulties with the product. He refused to allow Norman Spence accompany him to the meeting, but agreed to meet him later in the Tara Hotel.

'There he told me that due to further economies at the plant I was not needed anymore. He handed me a letter which he told me to bring home and read, and to put my feet up for a while. The letter was a note of dismissal on the grounds that I had not generated enough business. They offered me something like four weeks' redundancy pay.'

Spence refused to accept the conditions and then started yet another legal action for wrongful dismissal.

Spence says there followed efforts by a firm of consultants to justify getting rid of him.

In October 1982, the consultants produced a report, says Spence, which appeared to be at odds with the statements made in the company's grants and loan applications, also prepared by the same consultants. In this report Spence was blamed for losing the customers who threw out C&D for failing to deliver on time.

In another report, the consultants wrote 'no sales have yet been made outside the UK', ignoring the customers C&D had previously had in Switzerland, Denmark, Italy and Gibraltar, but had lost because of inability to supply or uncompetitiveness. The report also ignored the Dutch company, Hema, which C&D were supplying when the report was written, but which they lost for failure to deliver long after Spence had left. At the same time, the grant and loan applications prepared on C&D's behalf by the consultants stated 'a number of Continental customers exist'.

In yet another report in 1982 the consultants listed as an objective, 'Identify label designer and brief him on label design (for German market)', ignoring the fact that Spence had registered two brand names in Germany for C&D, 'Paddy' and 'Cara', as far back as 1977.

Meanwhile, Spence was contacted by a customer who owed C&D £8,000. Spence told the customer to send him the money as he was still a director, and then kept it himself along with a company Mercedes 280 he had been given.

'I rang C&D and told them I had the money and the car,' he says. 'They were furious and threatened to sue me. But I was still owed a lot of money by them.'

In the spring of 1984 Norman Spence received a notice to attend an Annual General Meeting of C&D on 13 March.

Spence acknowledged receipt of the notice of the AGM and directors' meeting, saying:

'I shall be delighted to attend this, the first properly constituted directors' meeting for more than eight years.

'Thank you also for the notice of the Annual General Meeting, the first properly constituted AGM for thirteen years . . . Please also let me have copies of the Accounts for the years ending 30 June 1975, 1976, 1977, 1978, 1979, 1980, 1981, 1982 and 1983.' (As a Director Spence would have been entitled to all annual accounts.)

'This obviously rang alarm bells at C&D,' says Spence, 'not only because of my letter, but because Albert had slipped up and had not had the notices worded correctly to achieve the only purpose for which the meeting had really been called, i.e. to get rid of me as a director.'

Spence subsequently received notice of a directors' meeting on 7 May 1984, to consider and pass the following resolution:

> That the Secretary be instructed to call an Extraordinary General Meeting to remove Norman Spence from the position of Director under the provisions of Section 182 of the *Companies Act 1963*.

Spence scribbled on his notice some notes on points he planned to raise at the meeting covering the alleged illegal use of materials banned under the terms of the EEC grant to C&D, and other matters.

But, in fact, he raised none of these matters. Instead at the beginning of the meeting he stated that it was not a directors' meeting because he was the only legally appointed director present. Neither Albert nor Kathleen Reynolds had been legally appointed directors, he said, nor was Michael Diffley the legally appointed Company Secretary.

'At first,' says Spence, 'I was ignored, and they carried on with the meeting. But I again interrupted. Albert said, "What are you talking about?" and told Diffley to carry on.'

Eventually Spence was handed a notice for an EGM on 5 June, 1984 to remove himself and Woolcock as directors.

Subsequently, company solicitor Patrick Groarke wrote to Spence stating that both Albert and Kathleen Reynolds were properly appointed directors, enclosing copies of Minutes of the meetings held in November and December 1975, at which Albert Reynolds had certified that Spence had sent his apologies. Spence says he was never advised of any such meeting.

On 31 May 1984, the shareholders Albert and Kathleen Reynolds requisitioned the directors Spence and Woolcock of C&D to convene an Extraordinary General Meeting of the company. Spence says it was very significant that he was requisitioned to convene the EGM, and he arranged the time, date and venue.

The agenda of the EGM was:

1. That Albert Reynolds be and is hereby ratified and confirmed as a Director of the Company.
2. That Kathleen Reynolds be and is hereby ratified and confirmed as a Director of the Company.
3. That Michael Diffley be and is hereby ratified and confirmed as Secretary of the Company.

4. That all actions taken by Albert and Kathleen Reynolds as Directors be and are hereby ratified.

5. That all actions taken by Michael Diffley as Secretary be and are hereby ratified.

6. That Norman Spence be and is hereby removed from the office of Director of C&D Foods Limited.

7. That Thomas Francis Woolcock be and is hereby removed from the office of Director of C&D Foods Limited.

Finally, on 31 July 1984, fifteen months after he had left the company, Norman Spence was removed as a director of C&D Foods.

In the meantime the company was in considerable difficulty and attempts were made to sell it.

In 1982 Norman Spence had dinner with the Chief Executive of AB Foods' manufacturing companies, Don Sanderson, who expressed an interest in C&D.

According to Spence, Albert Reynolds was very keen to sell, but didn't want to get involved in the negotiations. A number of meetings were held and good progress was reported.

Albert Reynolds wanted to retain an equity interest in the company, and Sanderson offered to give him some non-voting preference shares. 'Unfortunately,' says Spence, 'the whole deal fell apart when Reynolds refused to let Don Sanderson see the company's books until after he had named the price he would pay.'

Sanderson later travelled to Dublin to be a witness in Spence's case against C&D in October 1987.

In 1985 the giant Swiss group, Nestlé, was approached by the IDA and asked whether they had any interest in C&D.

Spence was contacted by Hugh Thomas, Nestlé's Vice-President in Switzerland, responsible for pet products, who told Spence about the IDA's approach, and asked him to act as a consultant in the purchase.

Later, however, Nestlé decided not to proceed, largely because C&D had no branded products.

In his subsequent legal action Spence claimed his sacking was wrong and in breach of an agreement reached on 23 February 1979. He said the agreement was that he would be employed until he reached his sixtieth birthday, which would occur in April 1992.

Among those who made a statement of support was former director Arthur McManus. He wrote: 'I can state without doubt that the company, its shareholders and directors were in agreement that a 10 per cent holding in the company's shares should be voted to Mr Spence.'

Eventually the matter reached the High Court in 1987 and was adjourned.

The judge said that while the case was set down for three days hearing, having looked at the papers he concluded it would take eight to ten days, and suggested both parties try to resolve the matter.

Spence came under pressure from his three counsel to settle. Part of their argument was that if he refused Reynolds' final offer (£90,000), and went into court and won, the matter could be appealed and stalled for another two years. Spence could not afford this and was made aware that the Industry Minister might well be Taoiseach by then.

He says he could not think clearly at the time as he shortly afterwards suffered his second heart attack, followed by a quadruple by-pass operation. So he settled.

Despite these problems business continued at C&D Petfoods.

By 1979 the company had moved to a turnover of £2,500,000 from £750,000 in 1974. It had made major investment in plant and machinery to take account of Sainsbury's draconian hygiene standards. Sainsbury's now accounted for 60 per cent of total output. Vets and chemists regularly arrived in Longford from London and every batch of food that left the factory was subjected to random tests at Sainsbury's own food laboratories.

Part of the reason for the success was Albert Reynolds' belief in his own products. He believed his products were more appealing to dogs and cats than those of his competitors because he used fresh offal collected from abattoirs around the country every day. Freezing offal tended to reduce the flavour, he claimed.

In one celebrated interview in *Business and Finance* magazine he told the reporter that the real test of petfood was if the manufacturer would taste it himself. He claimed to have done so.

Mervyn Mudd conceived the idea of a new plant which would have seven times the capacity of the existing one, and with new technology would reduce labour costs by almost 600 per cent. The price tag was £4,500,000.

Reynolds secured a FEOGA grant to the tune of £1,000,000. It was given on the basis that the factory was located in an underdeveloped area and the business was downstream agriculture and consequently had access to CAP funds.

The grant of £1,007,357 was approved by the EEC Commission on 22 December 1981. Reacting to the news Mr Reynolds said 'it would make a nice Christmas present', as well as helping to expand Continental sales into Germany, Switzerland and the Netherlands.

The IDA came up with another £500,000 and he put the remainder together with the aid of the ICC and AIB.

Albert Reynolds came in for criticism in the European Parliament where it was alleged that the grant was given because of his standing as a previous Government Minister. Official Unionist MEP John Taylor asked if Mr Reynolds' business connection was known at the time of the application – he had resigned as a director on being appointed Minister for Posts and Telegraphs in 1979.

In response Reynolds pointed out that he was the first person to make other Irish businessmen aware of EEC aid and if the Community had not paid up, then the IDA would have had to fork out another £500,000. Finally, he said it was the Coalition Government which was in power when the grant was approved and not Fianna Fáil.

Now out of power, Albert Reynolds decided to supervise the building of the new plant himself. But he had not bargained for three elections in two years and the matter of regular challenges to the Fianna Fáil leadership. Instead of supervising building contractors, he found himself back in power in 1982 as Minister for Industry and Energy selling gas to the British and struggling with a complicated Bula/Tara mining deal.

The plan was to have the new plant on stream by early 1982. But due to technical hitches it was more than a year late.

Now everything was done by computer, and staff had to be trained on the working of complicated equipment. The new plant was capable of producing three and a half times as much petfood in one shift as the old one could in two. But the company was losing money, staff were on a three-day week and new sales targets had not been achieved.

In a move first revealed by the *Sunday Press* in 1987, the State Rescue Agency, Fóir Teo, lent £500,000 to C&D in 1984 to safeguard jobs. In return it was allocated £500,000 redeemable cumulative preference shares at £1 each. (Cumulative preference shares normally have no voting rights, and in the case of Foir Teo were intended to be redeemable at par value out of future company profits. In effect, they amounted to a soft loan at 15% interest to tide the company over a difficult period.)

Interest payments from C&D, which amounted to £77,000, were paid in 1988 and 1989 when the ICC took over the interests of Fóir Teo following its abolition.

The chairman of Foir Teo was close Longford associate, Noel Hanlon. However, he had left the room when the decision was taken.

The terms of the soft loan, contained in a memo prepared by Fóir Teoranta confirm that £500,000 was to be repaid 'by six equal consequtive instalments commencing 31 December 1988'.

In March 1986 Foir Teoranta granted a further guarantee for £220,000 to C&D, bringing its total exposure to £720,000.

The audited accounts for the year ended 30.6.85 showed that at the time C&D had a net worth of £2.668 million. This was made up as follows:

	£
Shareholders	100,000
Shareholders loans	300,000
Other reserves	5,000
Foir Teo loan	500,000
Grants	1,763,000
Total	2,668,000

The figures show C&D had received a very high level of grants, but was in immediate need of finance. According to the Foir Teo memorandum 'in this scenario the company will be unlikely to survive'.

The intervention only came to light when legal documents were delivered to the Companies Office on 12 January 1987. Those returns showed that Albert Reynolds now owned 90,000 shares in the company and his wife, Kathleen, owned 10,000. They were the sole shareholders.

Albert Reynolds was back as a director again during the 1983/87 Coalition Government. The company had now begun a drive to sell 'own brands' to the smaller Irish supermarket chains. By 1985 they were supplying Quinnsworth, Tesco, Dunnes, Superquinn and Londis and hitting the big imported brand names by undercutting their prices.

The sales team also attacked and won markets in Italy, Denmark, Sweden and Switzerland. After Britain, Italy was Albert Reynolds' second biggest customer.

By the end of 1985 turnover at C&D was £7,400,000 of which £4,500,000 was export and £2,900,000 was home market and eighty-six staff were employed on a double shift roster. A figure of 1,700,000 cans per annum was reached.

A new contract was signed to supply the British hypermarket chain ASDA which had 110 retail outlets. This was valued at £1,600,000.

Writing in *The Irish Times* on 17 March, 1986, London Editor, Ella Shanahan, quoted Albert Reynolds as saying that it was estimated that 60 per cent of the grocery trade in Britain would be in the hands of four multiples by the end of the century – Sainsbury, Tesco, ASDA and Co-op. 'And I intend to be in three of them,' he added.

In addition the company was now marketing its own high quality *'Max'* label with some success.

But trouble was again looming. The renewed strength of the Punt against Sterling introduced more risk and cut already tight margins.

In April 1987, Mr Reynolds, now as Minister for Industry in the Fianna Fáil Government and no longer a director of C&D, went public to deny that the factory was in financial trouble. One of the reasons for the rumours was the decision by the company to factor out its debts to International Factors (Ireland) Ltd. Mr Reynolds said this was a normal business transaction which many companies engaged in to improve cash flow. The system is that the factoring company pays the manufacturer a fixed percentage for all the debts and then they are responsible for collecting the debts themselves.

But the factory survived the turbulent currency fluctuations and returned to profitability.

In 1988 it reported profits of £200,787 on a turnover of £9,800,000. The following year it recorded profits of £293,267 on a turnover of £10,000,000. In that year C&D Petfoods received approval for a £500,000 FEOGA grant for additional processing facilities. The announcement was made by the Minister for Agriculture, Michael O'Kennedy.

As a result of the investment in new equipment, the factory recorded pretax losses of £150,000 for 1990. The company also recorded a drop in sales as a result of the BSE or 'mad cow disease' scare.

In May 1990 Philip Reynolds, who by now was the second largest shareholder, was appointed Managing Director of the company, replacing Paul Dempsey who had managed the firm since December 1986.

The remuneration of the directors for 1988/'89, including Albert, Kathleen and Philip Reynolds was £108,000.

'The losses we suffered were a direct result of an investment we made,' Philip told *Business and Finance* magazine. 'We invested £2,800,000 in new technology, but there were some problems in setting it up. It cost us dearly in the short term, but we will have longer term benefits.'

This technology concentrated on new easy-open soft packages. The first contract for this product came from Carrefour in France, and similar business followed in Belgium, Italy, Norway and Sweden.

In 1990 C&D also launched a new range of petfoods in association with the US Petfood giant, Ralstan Purina. Purina is one of the biggest petfood producers in the world.

Relations with the workforce, which now numbers 135, have been relatively good, although the wages are low in the petfood industry.

In 1982, for example, the Labour Court was told that the rates at C&D were among the lowest in the region. The Court recommended higher wages, the company accepted the increase, but the workers rejected it as too low. Inevitably, there was publicity about a Minister for Industry paying low wages.

There was even more publicity when RTE newsreader Charles Mitchell unwittingly crossed the picket line as a passenger in a car when was picking up food for his wife's beagles.

In all there have been three strikes at the plant since it opened.

'Albert Reynolds was a fair employer, but there were ongoing problems with wages and conditions,' says SIPTU official Bob Brady, who negotiated with C&D management from 1985-90, but is now based in Monaghan. (Mr Brady sailed into more turbulent waters during the Hanlon ambulance dispute.)

In 1993 C&D claimed inability to pay the final phase of the PESP on time. Instead it was postponed for six months.

At the time of Albert Reynolds' appointment as Taoiseach, Philip reported that they were doing business with 80 per cent of the abattoirs in Ireland. They imported twenty trailers of cans each week, and exported them back full. He also reported that they were looking at possible acquisitions, not necessarily within Ireland. This strategy was aimed at increasing the rate of growth in Europe and beyond. Philip Reynolds predicted that the company was in a position to pay between £3,000,000 - £4,000,000 for the right company.

'This is a most extraordinary claim,' says PD Deputy, Michael McDowell, 'given the fact that C&D could not pay PESP in 1993 despite the £1,000,000 Masri investment in March 1992.'

Again the company was investing in new facilities, this time in extended warehousing and cold storage.

The most recent documents filed in the Companies Office for the year ending 31 December 1991 show Albert Reynolds as the largest shareholder with 164,000 ordinary shares; his wife Kathleen with 40,000; their son Philip with 156,000; and their second son, Albert Junior with 40,000.

Foir Teoranta, the former State rescue agency, is listed as still owning 500,000 redeemable cumulative preference shares. On Tuesday 14 June 1994 Albert Reynolds officially told the Dáil that he held a 41 per cent shareholding in the family business.

C&D Foods hit the national news headlines unexpectedly in May 1994 when it was revealed that two Arabs had been granted Irish passports for investing £1,100,000 in C&D Foods through the use of the little known Business Migration Scheme.

Under the terms of the *Irish Nationality and Citizenship Act 1956* the Minister for Justice may grant a passport to a foreigner if he/she has what are termed 'Irish associations'.

What exactly 'Irish associations' means is not clearly defined, and the issue was the subject of much debate in the Dáil in March 1956. During that debate a Fianna Fáil Deputy, Michael O'Morain, said that an 'Arab who drinks Irish whiskey' could claim 'Irish associations'.

In 1986 the little used mechanism was revived as a means of attracting foreign investment into Ireland through the Business Migration Scheme. Similar schemes operate in many other countries, notably Canada and Australia.

Government policy since 1986 had been to allow naturalisation where a foreign national made a substantial investment – over £500,000 – in a job creation investment scheme and bought a residence in the Republic. A typical rule of thumb in official circles appeared to be that each £1,000,000 should create twenty new jobs.

The attraction for the Irish company was obvious. They received the funds at a reduced interest rate of as low as 3 or 5 per cent.

From the investor's point of view the attraction was the Irish passport which allowed him or her free movement around the twelve member states of the European Community. In most cases the investor would seek to ensure that the loan was repaid, often through some kind of preferential share which would give first call on the company's assets. Where the assets were inadequate, the company would have to invest a large proportion of the money in a bank, but would be left with the benefit of some costless capital.

In the past the Industrial Development Authority, now Forbairt, provided letters to some project promoters confirming that they had qualified for grant-aid, and would benefit from further finance. This was an important factor for both the investor and the Government.

A number of accountancy and legal firms also became involved as 'marriage brokers' between the investors and the Irish companies.

News that Arab businessman, Khalid Sabih Masri, and Najwa Sabih Taher Masri, were both granted Irish citizenship on 15 December 1992 was published in *Iris Oifigiuil.*

But on 30 July 1993 *Phoenix* magazine highlighted the fact that the Masri application had been supported by the Minister for the Environment, Michael Smith, 'from personal knowledge of, and intimate acquaintance with him and to vouch for his good character'. Michael Smith was a close confidante of Albert Reynolds along with Pádraig Flynn, who as Minister for Justice approved the citizenship application. The three had all been sacked from ministerial office by former Taoiseach Charles Haughey in November 1991 when they supported a motion calling for his resignation.

The Masri application was approved by Justice Minister Flynn, now EC Commissioner, during the period of a Fianna Fáil minority Government following the resignation of the Progressive Democrats from office.

The matter was laid to rest until Sunday 22 May 1994, when *Sunday Independent* Business Editor Martin Fitzpatrick pointed out that the petfood family business of the Taoiseach had benefited from an investment in the scheme. A spokesman for the Taoiseach told the paper 'he never comments on matters relating to family business'.

This was clearly not the case as he had done so in April 1987.

The story, although consigned to page three of the *Sunday Independent,* immediately took off with questions being raised as to whether internal departmental guidelines on residency and equity investment had been flouted in this case. (The Masris have a Dublin address at 11 Rawson Court, Haddington Road, but appear to spend little time there.) The IDA later confirmed that the bulk of the passport investments – approximately twenty a year since 1986 – were in fact loans at bargain basement rates.

The Progressive Democrats quickly branded the Business Migration Scheme the 'Passports-for-Sale' scheme.

Party Deputy Michael McDowell immediately tabled a series of Dáil questions to the Taoiseach for the following Tuesday, 24 May. The questions were disallowed, but in a skilful parliamentary move

McDowell, a distinguished Senior Counsel, drafted a Private Member's Bill, forcing a Dáil debate for ten minutes a week later. The Bill sought to revoke the Masri citizenship unless they made a declaration of loyalty to the State in open court by 31 July.

In a bid to counter the attack the Government granted a full Dáil debate in advance of McDowell's Bill with the Minister for Justice, Maire Geoghegan-Quinn, insisting that all legal requirements had been complied with in the Masri case.

She revealed that Khalid Masri and Najwa Masri were in fact a mother and son, and not husband and wife, as had been believed. She also confirmed that the Arabs had made the required Declaration of Fidelity to the Nation and Loyalty to the State in the District Court in accordance with the law.

The Minister said that Khalid Masri Senior had subsequently invested £1,500,000 in a forestry project which created an estimated fifty jobs and had indicated that a further £1,500,000 would be made available for another venture. 'On this basis I am prepared to grant naturalisation to him,' she declared.

She added that as the Department of Justice had no method of follow-up to these cases she had set up a committee to make recommendations on the Business Migration Scheme.

In her speech Minister Geoghegan-Quinn asked Deputy McDowell if he was aware that the scheme for granting citizenship had been in operation when two of his colleagues were in the Cabinet, and that one of them had wanted it extended to cover golf clubs. (Fianna Fáil sources told political journalists that the golf club incident related to Ballyneety in the heart of PD leader Des O'Malley's East Limerick constituency, but that O'Malley's request for a passport had been turned down by the Fianna Fáil Minister for Justice.)

'Publish what you like, I will not be intimidated,' replied McDowell in a heated Dáil exchange.

'What kind of squalid little banana republic, with a Papa Doc Duvalier regime have we when that is the treatment we give?' he asked.

The tense Dáil debate took an unexpected turn when Deputy Pat Rabbitte of Democratic Left produced an eyebrow-raising document, from an international lawyer, which described Ireland as 'Greenland' for the purposes of secrecy.

Anyone from China or the Indian sub-Continent was not welcome to invest in Ireland, but an investor from the Middle East might succeed. The whole process of obtaining a visa could be gone through in just one day for a fee of £25,000, according to the document.

Deputy Rabbitte suggested that the whole scheme sounded more like a money-laundering operation with racist overtones than a legitimate investment scheme.

On 29 May *Sunday Independent* reporter Sam Smyth revealed that the Masri citizenship deal had been brokered by a Roscommon-based architect and businessman, Brian O'Carroll, and American consultant, Rick Malone.

O'Carroll has long-standing Fianna Fáil connections. Former Minister of State Terry Leyden was once a draughtsman in his company, and he is friendly with the Reynolds family.

Lyden, while a Minister of State, had brought Khalid Masri into Leinster House and introduced him to the then Taoiseach, Charles Haughey.

Rick Malone is an Irish-American lawyer who was one of the main players in promoting the investment and residency scheme.

Khalid Masri Senior was identified as the chairman of the Arab Supply and Trading Company in Riyadh, the largest food processor in Saudi Arabia. It later emerged that Minister Michael Smith had been introduced to Khalid Masri Senior by Brian O'Carroll who knew him through the Minister's architect brother, Jim.

Brian O'Carroll told the *Sunday Business Post* that he 'doesn't think' he ever mentioned the name of C&D Foods to Smith. The Minister insisted he simply passed on the application without even a covering note to the Minister for Justice.

In an apparent mix-up, it was Masri's wife and son who were naturalised rather than his wife and daughter which was what was intended.

Later, the international lawyer who handles business for the Masri family, Fadi Malouf, said he would have preferred another company when he heard of the political connections of C&D, but was told it would be 'all right'.

On 30 May in an attempt to end the growing controversy the Taoiseach's son, Philip Reynolds, Managing Director of C&D Foods, issued a statement confirming the investment of £1,100,000 which had resulted 'in the creation of approximately forty jobs'.

In his statement Philip Reynolds said that at no time during the negotiations was the issue of naturalisation of passports discussed, 'nor was any such condition applied to our commercial transaction'.

But the episode came at a highly embarrassing time for the Government, just as it was about to launch a new Ethics in Public Office Bill, and in the run-up to the European elections and two by-elections in Mayo West and Dublin South Central.

On 31 May the Tánaiste and Labour leader Dick Spring had a 'long and frank discussion' on the matter with the Taoiseach and Minister for Justice. In an unusual step Mr Spring asked to see the Department of Justice files himself and concluded that the matter was conducted 'in an ethical, above-board and arms-length way'.

Mr Spring confirmed that he was satisfied that no representations had been made by the Taoiseach, and there was no knowledge to suggest that the Minister for the Environment, Michael Smith, knew the identity of the firm receiving the investment, although that information was known to the Justice Minister, Pádraig Flynn.

The Tánaiste added that in order to ensure total transparency in the future, recommendations from the working group examining the Business Migration Scheme would be placed on a statutory basis. An annual report would be laid before both Houses of the Oireachtas.

A major part of the controversy centred on the Taoiseach's insistence that he had no knowledge of the investment in his company, despite the fact that he is a major shareholder and his wife and son both directors.

'I don't know this family. I never met them. I know nothing about them,' he insisted.

While in Opposition he said he had been a non-executive director and chaired some meetings, but was not directly involved in the day-to-day running of the business. He resigned as director each time he was appointed Minister, most recently on 10 March 1987.

On Sunday night, 5 June, fresh fax sheets started to arrive in the newsrooms of the national newspapers in Dublin.

PD Deputy Michael McDowell had now got hold of the most recent C&D returns to the Companies Office which showed that during 1991, even while he was Minister for Finance, Albert Reynolds had received an additional 51,250 ordinary shares in the company. The returns also showed that at the end of 1991 C&D was indebted by £1,400,000, just months before the Masris made their investment of £1,100,000.

Government sources reacted by saying that Michael McDowell could continue to 'throw mud' at the Taoiseach, but it would not stick.

Answering questions later in the Dáil, the Taoiseach asked why a 'different set of rules' should apply to a company run by his son. He said the country's reputation had also been denigrated in an insulting and demeaning manner.

'No true patriot would talk of his country in some of the terms that have been used,' he said.

While the controversy appeared to have some impact in the subsequent elections, where Fianna Fáil lost both by-elections and Labour's vote decreased dramatically, it was, ironically, Labour who appeared to suffer the most.

Getting into the fast lane. Albert Reynolds tries out a racing motor-cycle at a show in the mid '70s.

Campaigning in Longford with former Taoiseach Jack Lynch in the 1977 General Election.

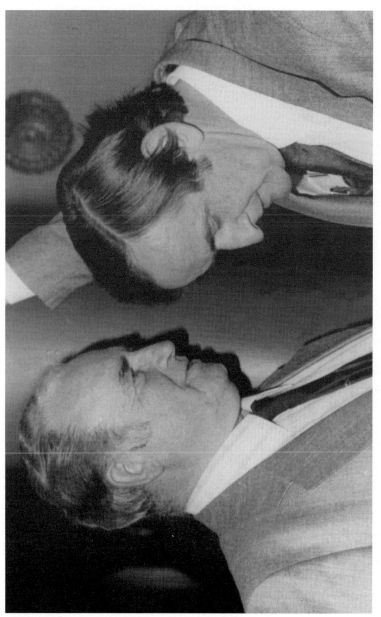

Getting a word of advice. Albert Reynolds with former Independent TD Joe Sheridan at the 1977 election count.

Those who ate Kathleen's cheesecake. Left to right: Tony Carberry, James Coyle, James Doaler, Ned 'the County' Reilly, Albert Reynolds, Michael McCarthy, Minister for Health Charles Haughey, Noel Hanlon, Noel McGeeney, Tony Egan, Tommy Breaden, Paddy Farrell.

Sales Talk. Minister of State for Industry, Ray Burke, spells out the benefits of C & D 'Paddy' cat food at a London Trade Fair in 1979. On his right is Norman Spence marketing manager of C & D.

Albert Reynolds, Minister for Posts and Telegraphs, lays the foundation stone for a new post office in Mullingar in June 1981.

Enter Albert stage right. Albert Reynolds arriving for a Fianna Fáil press conference during the November 1982 General Election. (Derek Speirs/Report).

June 28th 1982

Norman Spence Esq.,
Mountain House,
Llanteg,
Norberth,
Pembrokeshire,
WALES.

RE: C & D Foods Ltd.

Dear Norman

I regret the delay in formally replying to your letter of
27th March, but no doubt you will appreciate how busy I have
been since then, and in any event, I dealt with all the
matters you raised in my last telephone conversation with
you.

3. The necessary borrowings and grants have been organised
    by our accountants internal and external and management
    consultants employed from January 1981 to advise and
    support the general management function.

4. Yet sales are now running at only 13,000 cases per week
    and the company is now making a serious loss.

5. Clearly, irrespective of the minor day to day hiccups
    of the type discussed in your letter,

    (a) Production management has done its job.

    (b) Financial and general management has done its job.

    (c) Sales management - i.e. you - have not done your
         job.

Accordingly, it has been necessary to

    (i)   Introduce a new management structure reporting to
          Michael Diffley.

    (ii) Employ sales and marketing consultants to ensure
          the proper and planned marketing of our products.

    (iii) Set budgets and targets for all management.

Yours faithfully

Albert Reynolds

Extracts from letter written by Albert Reynolds to Norman Spence, 28 June 1982.

An IMS poll in the *Sunday Independent* on 5 June showed that only one-third of the electorate was satisfied with the accounts offered by Albert Reynolds and other Government Ministers, with Labour supporters particularly upset at the revelations.

The outcome of the entire saga left the Masris less than impressed. In an RTE interview on 2 June, Minister Michael Smith said the family had cancelled future investments in the country.

The passport controversy refused to go away. It dominated the first Dáil debate on the new Ethics in Public Office Bill on 23 June.

In a trenchant speech Michael McDowell again attacked the Labour Party and the media.

'He (Albert Reynolds) personally gained more than any other person from the Masris' £1,000,000 loan. As the largest single beneficiary of this loan, he has a brass neck to say this is his family's private matter. We are concerned with his political ethics, of which we find precious little trace in recent events,' he said.

Deputy McDowell said *The Irish Times* was so afraid of telling its readers the truth that it even refused to print a statement based largely on the company's records for fear of libelling the Taoiseach, who had already taken them for a significant amount in libel damages.

In a particularly virulent attack on the Labour leader, Dick Spring, Deputy McDowell accused him of being 'morally brain dead' in his reaction to the controversy.

Fianna Fáil's Batt O'Keeffe replied by branding McDowell as the 'Dáil's football hooligan in pin stripes'.

During the debate Minister of State, Eithne FitzGerald, promised an amendment, to be introduced at committee stage, to cover actions by one Minister which could benefit another but did not require a Cabinet decision.

On 1 July during the Dáil Adjournment Debate, Michael McDowell returned yet again to the passport controversy, repeating his allegations that the Taoiseach was the personal beneficiary of £1,000,000 investment made by way of a 'soft loan' to the Longford company, C&D Foods.

'We are asked to believe that two strangers who never resided here, before or since, made a gratuitous, non-commercial loan to an Irish company, and that nobody involved knew or suspected that the purpose of the loan was to obtain Irish – and therefore EU – citizenship,' he told the House.

In August 1994 it was revealed that C&D Foods had repeatedly discharged illegal levels of pollution into a local stream at Edgeworthstown. The stream flows into the River Black, a tributary of the Inny.

Longford County Council records showed that the company breached six separate conditions of its licence to discharge waste during 1993. In one sample the concentration of ammonia was found to be 164 times greater than permitted.

The factory's pollution licence, issued by Longford County Manager, Michael Killeen, in February 1988, allows it to discharge 'trade and sewage effluent' into the headwaters of the River Black, via a field drain at the rear of the premises, subject to a total of fourteen specific conditions.

C&D's Managing Director, Philip Reynolds, said the pollution problem had resulted from the firm's growth, but added that it would be solved early in 1995 when the factory was connected to a new sewage plant for the town.

Greenpeace Ireland, who obtained the figures from Longford County Council, explained that the information on C&D had been obtained as part of a major inquiry by the organisation into the incidence of pollution throughout the Republic. This had shown that many companies in the agri-business sector had 'scant regard for environmental protection laws'.

County Manager, Michael Killeen, admitted that while there were grounds for prosecuting the firm, no legal action had been taken.

'With work in progress on the sewage works, the likelihood is that any prosecution would be adjourned pending the completion,' he said. 'There seemed to be no point in incurring legal costs.'

****

Meanwhile, the outlook for the petfood market is excellent.

Ireland, for example, with little over three million people, now spends £2,800,000 a year feeding its 600,000 dogs and 400,000 cats. Scale that up in countries the size of France and Germany, and the potential becomes clear.

To cater for the more discerning cats and dogs, C&D diversified and can now offer such delights as turkey and salmon, rabbit and game, beef and heart, or rabbit and kidney. These dainty dishes were developed in association with the National Food Centre.

'Because we're smaller than our main rivals, Spillers Petfoods and Pedigree Petfoods, we can be more flexible,' Albert Reynolds told *Sunday Press* journalist Brenda Power in 1990. 'Like introducing those new "ice-cream" tubs, for example. That's what the customers want, and they're the ones you have to look after.'

In January 1994 the *Checkout Yearbook* predicted major growth in the sector. The greatest growth will be in cat food, but the market for dog food is also expected to increase, though at a slower rate.

The Irish are the highest per capita dog owners in Europe with 45 per cent of homes having a dog, and 21 per cent a cat.

But only 35 per cent of Irish dogs are fed a prepared food compared to 80 per cent in Germany.

One of the major reasons for the growth in the petfood market is the increase in the use of convenience foods and more food eaten away from home, leaving fewer scraps for the family pet.

Whether they buy or not, Philip Reynolds, in true political style, insists that the factory will always remain in Co Longford where his father and Matty Lyons set it up on a shoestring twenty-four years ago.

In the petfood business Albert Reynolds' motto was always: 'Look after the customer'.

If you looked after the customer and gave the best deal you could, then the customer would buy your Mars bars, your petfood, would dance on your paraffin-soaked floors . . . and would vote you back into office again and again and again . . .

– 6 –

The Newspaper King

June 15, 1990. Guests arrived for a reception at the new offices of the *Longford News* on Dublin Street. The official opening was to be performed by the Minister for Finance, Albert Reynolds, who once owned the paper.

A free press is well worth the occasional irritation it causes to people in authority, the Minister told the assembled gathering.

'A free press goes hand in hand with freedom of opinion and freedom of expression, and I wouldn't have it any other way.'

The local newspapers, he said, had an indispensable role in Irish life as documents of record. They provided an enduring chronicle of local affairs and a valuable forum for discussion and analysis of the things that matter in a community.

'I have been around long enough to know that criticism – and sometimes unfair criticism – is part of the currency of public life and one learns to ride with the punches,' he declared.

Whatever about the mixed metaphor, punches or no punches, one of the things Albert Reynolds made clear when he became Taoiseach was he would have no hesitation in issuing legal proceedings against any newspaper which he felt defamed his character or reputation.

In July '92 he told political correspondents that he would take legal action against any newspaper which impugned his personal integrity. He confirmed that a number of such actions were in train.

'I have a simple, straightforward philosophy,' he declared. 'Don't tell me lies or don't tell lies on me using twisted facts. Just tell the truth. This has nothing to do with me as Taoiseach, but it has everything to do with me as Albert Reynolds.'

Later it was revealed that the Taoiseach had agreed a settlement with *The Irish Times* in relation to an article written by economist Raymond Crotty, in which he had suggested that Albert Reynolds had abused his Cabinet position by obtaining EC funds to assist in the establishment of C&D Petfoods.

The paper acknowledged that there was no foundation for this inference and published a front page apology. The offending article was published as part of *The Irish Times* opinion page in the run-up to the Maastricht Referendum.

An action against the *Sunday Tribune* in connection with an article on the Beef Tribunal was dropped following the publication of a correction which, Mr Reynolds said, 'got the facts right, straightaway'.

This new defensive approach was in stark contrast to the previous Taoiseach, Charles Haughey, who, although he had been maligned many times in numerous articles and magazines, chose not to sue while he held the office.

But that was all a far cry from the day in 1973 when Albert Reynolds decided to buy the *Longford News*.

For a small town, Longford was remarkable in constantly maintaining two newspapers, starting in the early nineteenth century.

The *Longford Messenger*, founded in 1838, the *Longford Journal* (1839), the *Midland Counties Gazette* (1853) and the *Longford Independent* (1868) were among the first to appear, and their survival rate was quite good.

These were followed by the *Longford Leader* (1897), the *Longford News* (1936) and the *Longford Telegraph* (1948). Also, owing to its geographical location, Co Longford is included in the circulation area of adjoining county newspapers.

The *Longford News* was founded by Vincent Gill, one of the most eccentric people ever to enter Irish journalism. Having spent some time in the army and the Gardaí, he returned to Longford to set up a paper on the most limited means.

For the first thirty years Gill ran the paper single-handedly, often making up news stories when he was short of copy, along with devising the most outrageous system of getting advertising.

In his book *Paper Tigers* Hugh Oram quotes Derek Cobbe, who succeeded Gill as editor, on some of Gill's schemes.

'For example, in an issue he would tell the courting couple on the canal line last week that if they didn't take out a subscription for the paper, their names would appear next week. Often seven or eight subscriptions were taken out the following week.'

Albert Reynolds had memories, too, of Vincent Gill: 'There was a time, of course, when Vincent wrote all sorts of things about the local gossip. I mean he had a gossip column that was dangerous to say the least. If you ended up in it, everybody knew what your private life was all about. He wrote about chaps who went to dances going home with somebody's daughter or maybe somebody's wife or whatever. As he said himself, there was no point in suing him, there was nothing to get. But he often ended up at the bottom of the canal in Longford.'

Derek Cobbe gives another example: 'There was an itinerant wedding in Longford which attracted a large attendance. Vince listed the entire diplomatic corps from the President down as being at the wedding. But then equally if there was a society wedding in town, he listed every single itinerant from near and far as being present at the wedding. Even at St Mel's College past pupils' reunion dinner, he listed everybody he knew from Longford who had ever stayed in Mountjoy Prison as being at the dinner, and had them listed as being out for the occasion.'

Frequently, when he was short of news, Gill would borrow a whole page of news from the *Leitrim Observer*, or some other paper, to fill up the space. Once he printed a full page in black with the caption: 'Blackout in Drumlish'.

His home, Harbour Row, was his office which he shared with his dogs and cats. His pets came first and cat food and dog food came far higher on the list than printing ink.

'He was known for his cats and dogs,' said Albert Reynolds. 'He always had five or six cats and three or four dogs in the van with him. He wrote the paper and produced it with the help of a young McCrainer lad in Longford and he distributed it himself. He collected whatever money he wanted to keep him and the paper going or to pay for the newsprint or for a few local schoolboys to deliver the paper around the town.'

So widespread was Vincent Gill's reputation that he was featured on BBC's *Panorama* programme.

As he grew old Vincent Gill, who died in 1976, did not want the inevitable to happen – the *Leader* to buy the *News* simply to close it down. He wanted his life's work to continue.

Gill asked local shopkeeper Dessie Hynes if he was interested in buying the paper. Dessie said he probably was, and paid a deposit of £1,000, before heading for Listowel Races. At the races he met Albert Reynolds and convinced him to buy the paper. When they returned, a cheque in Albert's name was exchanged for Dessie's at the solicitor's office.

The price was around £12,000, which included the much neglected cottage at Harbour Row.

Now a newspaper proprietor, Albert Reynolds had neither the time nor experience to run his latest acquisition and hired a free-lance reporter, Eugene McGee, a native of North Longford.

McGee was acting editor until a new broom, Derek Cobbe, joined. He had been a director and editor of the rival *Longford Leader*, but left when he accused the owner Lucius Farrell of allegedly bugging the telephones.

Derek Cobbe was a very different, but no less colourful, editor than Vincent Gill.

Conscious of the paper's history, Cobbe once ran a story that Longford was about to pull out of the EEC. The paper carried a picture of Longford with a wall across it, and another picture of the cathedral being taken down to be moved elsewhere as the bishop wished to remain within the Common Market.

Derek Cobbe came from a working-class background in Dublin where his mother still lives. Having trained as a printer he won a scholarship to the United States and set up his own printing business which, unfortunately, was destroyed by fire. It was uninsured. He was also involved in showbusiness and having returned from America travelled around Ireland for the summer with his friends, the Duffy's Circus family, as a bill poster.

In 1969 he became production manager of the *Longford Leader*, then general manager, editor and director until he left in 1974 to join the *Longford News*, now owned by Albert Reynolds.

Apart from newspapers, Cobbe was always full of ideas. He once printed 10,000 badges for a customer in Kerry, anticipating that the county would win five All-Ireland football titles in-a-row. The slogan read: 'Kerry, five-in-a-row'. However, Kerry was dramatically beaten by Offaly, so Cobbe overprinted the badges to read: 'Kerry, five-in-a-row. Ha, Ha.' He sold the badges like hot cakes in Co Offaly.

Derek Cobbe's deal with Albert Reynolds was that he be appointed editor and joint Managing Director with him, and be given a small shareholding in the *Longford News*, rising with performance results. Sales were at fewer than 2,000 copies, so it was a hard slog.

Albert and Kathleen Reynolds lent a hand in the early days.

'I hadn't the same ways and means of doing things as Vincent Gill had,' Reynolds told Hugh Oram. 'First of all, I wasn't in the business of writing columns. In the early days of the paper after I bought it, I think it was the first Saturday it came out, we had nobody to distribute it, so we had to work all night on Friday, and my wife Kathleen had to distribute the earlier editions. Before the shops opened on a Saturday morning, she was going around the town and the county at about 5.00 am or 6.00 am. It was a family affair at that stage.'

Cobbe's first task was to insist on moving out of Harbour Row and into new premises.

'The smell of the cats and dogs, you just couldn't stick it,' he said.

The paper moved into Breaden's old bakery on Dublin Street and set up shop. Cobbe bought a second-hand Cossar printing press from the *Imperial Reporter* in Enniskillen.

Albert Reynolds rarely appeared at the newspaper other than to sign the cheques.

'Both our signatures were supposed to be on the cheques,' Derek Cobbe remembers. 'However, as I could rarely find Albert I learned to do an impeccable reproduction of his signature.'

However, by this time Albert Reynolds had become a County Councillor and later a Dáil Deputy in 1977. The paper was constantly accused of leaning favourably towards Albert Reynolds.

'Frank Hall in his TV programme used to poke fun at how many pictures of Albert Reynolds we would use. So in one issue I put in fifty-two photographs of him, one for every week in the year, just to get it up for Hall,' says Cobbe. 'Albert Reynolds never interfered in the news, but was constantly accused of doing so by Fine Gael members of Longford County Council.'

Soon the results began to show. After a year under the Reynolds/Cobbe stewardship, the sales of the paper increased to 4,000, a rise of 100 per cent.

Journalist Liam Collins went to work for the *News* in 1974. He had never heard of Albert Reynolds before. Outside of the ballroom circuit, few had.

'Clearing out Vincent Gill's things in Harbour Row – drawers full of unopened letters, scandalous pictures, bundles of back-issues of his beloved *Longford News* and stacks of the *New Yorker* magazine to which he contributed the odd witty line – I first met Albert Reynolds,' wrote Collins in a booklet to commemorate the thirty-eighth Longford Association Dinner Dance at which Albert Reynolds was honoured.

'Tanned, wearing a well-cut suit and stepping out of his deep blue Daimler car, he was the epitome of the successful businessman. The new owner of the *News* said "hello" and exchanged a bit of banter. Then he left us to get on with the job in hand.

'Gradually I came to know the dynamic go-getter of Longford, listening to the hair-raising stories Albert told about himself, or sitting in Peter Clarke's hearing about him from Barney Willis who was his gardener at the time, the eccentric but lovable Jimmy Molloy who ran the *Musical Gazette*, and indeed from many others who saw something special even in those early days. There was something about him, a feeling that this guy was going places.'

Liam Collins, now with the *Sunday Independent*, wrote that it was to Albert Reynolds' credit that he never interfered in the running of the *News*.

'Always one to improvise, he used to claim it was "against National Union of Journalists' rules" to leave out a court case when less than sober locals called to his door in the small hours after closing time.'

Collins admits that the *News* was definitely pro-Fianna Fáil and did help Albert Reynolds on his way to Dáil Éireann. But being who he was, Albert Reynolds would have generated many news column inches anyway.

Under the editorial direction of Derek Cobbe the *News* continued to expand. And there was no shortage of wild and wonderful stories. Journalist Alan O'Keeffe who worked there from 1977 to 1980 once wrote about the 'Killoe sheepdog' who was a musical fan but didn't like Larry Cunningham.

'He seemed to enjoy a wide variety of singers, pop, country and traditional. But when Larry began to sing, that dog would twist his head to one side, growl and bark. But give that animal Joe Dolan, and you had one contented canine.'

But the life of the publisher and the politician did not go hand in hand. One person reportedly went to Albert Reynolds' home on twelve separate occasions to try and keep a report out of the *News*. Finally, he decided to sell it.

The paper was sold to the *Meath Chronicle* in a £100,000 plus deal, which included a printing contract. Derek Cobbe remained on as editor. The new owner was John (Jack) T Davis, while his brother James, the editor of the *Chronicle*, became the other shareholder. The acquisition gave the Davis brothers a clear run of Meath and Longford, as well as taking in parts of Westmeath and Cavan.

Cobbe, however, in turn, bought the *News* back from the *Chronicle* in 1983. At the time journalists in the rival *Longford Leader* were locked in a bitter dispute with the editor, Lucius Farrell, and this was an added bonus for Cobbe. In 1990, he sold the paper to the *Leitrim Observer*.

The *Observer* sold it to its current owners, the *Midland Tribune* group. It is now a sister paper of the *Roscommon Champion* and continues to thrive under the editorship of Paul Healy.

A former employee of the *News*, Eugene McGee, is now the editor of its rival, the *Longford Leader*. Derek Cobbe has since left the newspaper business, but continues to live in Longford.

But without the intervention of Albert Reynolds there might not be a *Longford News* today.

'Had he not bought it, then it certainly would not have survived as an independent publication,' Derek Cobbe confirms.

– 7 –

The Night of the Short Knives

Sunday, 21 May, 1977. Journalist Liam Collins was sitting in the bar of the Greville Arms in Granard, Co Longford, enjoying a quiet pint after closing time with the editor of the *Longford News*, Derek Cobbe, and a local man, Packie Finnan.

Suddenly, news came through that Albert Reynolds had beaten the sitting Fianna Fáil TD, Frank Carter, at a convention in Mullingar earlier that night. It was a sensational piece of news. Collins immediately got on the telephone to the Dublin papers to make a few extra shillings with a couple of paragraphs outlining the significance of the event.

'Who is this Albert Reynolds anyway?' the papers asked. 'And what has this Longford squabble got to do with the important things in Dublin?'

But the breakthrough on that Sunday night was what Albert Reynolds had been waiting for, and gave him the opening he needed. Albert Reynolds had come from an apolitical family. Politics were never discussed at home while he was growing up, although his parents generally voted for the two local Fianna Fáil TDs.

His first knowledge of politics came in Summerhill College where a number of his schoolmates would have come from strong Fianna Fáil families.

'It seemed to me at the time that Fianna Fáil was the party to do things,' he later told the *Sunday Tribune*.

His interest in politics began rather as a hobby which emerged alongside the ballroom business. He rented out halls to the political parties for functions and got to know some of the key people.

'You'd be all over the country, in Athy, Tipperary and Galway, dealing with political organisations, gradually getting to know them.'

One of those he got to know well was Neil Blaney, then a prominent Fianna Fáil Minister, who ran a sort of flying by-election team.

'I became part of that team and that's where the first excitement of politics came to me. You worked like hell for two weeks, wherever the by-election was.'

Reynolds was part of a well organised by-election task force throughout the '60s and was heavily involved, for example, in the election of Gerry Collins in Limerick West in 1967 and Des O'Malley in Limerick East in 1968. But he had always confined his politics to election times.

'That was me, I was in there, and gone,' he said of the period.

But during all this time one of the most important influences in shaping Albert Reynolds' thinking was the quiet, sombre Independent Deputy for Longford/Westmeath, Joe Sheridan.

Now retired and living outside Mullingar, Joe Sheridan humbly plays down the influence he had on the budding Taoiseach.

Having been rejected by a Fine Gael convention, Joe ran as an Independent and was elected at every election from 1961 until 1981 when he decided to stand down.

He was a powerful figure during the Lemass Government of 1965/69 when Fianna Fáil did not have an overall majority and relied on the support of a few Independents. His strength of support was seen in the next general election in 1969 when he headed the poll with 7,133 first preference votes. He headed the poll again subsequently in the 1977 general election.

When Joe Sheridan decided to contest the election as an Independent, the first two people to come and offer help were Jimmy O'Brien from Lanesboro and Albert Reynolds. Reynolds acted as Director of Elections for Sheridan.

'I was based a lot in the Longford Arms Hotel at that time and Albert had his office there running the ballroom business,' Joe recalls.

From the start Joe says he could see that Albert knew as much about politics as himself. One of the first things Albert said to Joe was: 'Have you a map of the constituency, Joe? The first thing you need is a map.' The idea of a map had never crossed Joe Sheridan's mind before.

When going to Dublin, Albert and Joe would sometimes travel together.

'Albert often drove me to Dublin and he spent a lot of time hanging around the Dáil. He was a desperate smoker that time and he always seemed to have loads of cigarettes. But often he would be talking so much on the way to Dublin that he would run out of petrol. But we had great times going up and down.'

There is little doubt but that Joe Sheridan kindled a love of active politics in Albert Reynolds and it was while on those trips to Dublin that he decided politics might be an option.

Albert Reynolds was elected as the constituency representative from Longford/Westmeath to the Fianna Fáil National Executive, a useful but low-profile post. He served as the Longford delegate from 1971 to 1974. In 1973 he was appointed Director of Elections for Fianna Fáil in Longford.

But a key development was his selection as President of Longford Chamber of Commerce in 1972. This was his vital stepping stone into public life and gave him an appetite to represent the people.

He quickly immersed himself in projects such as the development of an airport at Abbeyshrule. When Longford Aviation Airfield Development Ltd held a meeting to discuss the idea of an airfield at Abbeyshrule in January 1977, members of the public took shares totalling £40,000.

'I was happy enough with that (the Chamber of Commerce), but then the local Fianna Fáil organisation and the sitting TD, Frank

Carter, asked me to stand for the County Council which I did. I topped the poll with a quota and a half,' he said.

In June 1974 the following pen picture appeared in the *Longford Leader*:

'Going forward in the Longford electoral area and contesting the local elections for the first time, Albert Reynolds is well known in the business world, and is Secretary of the County Executive of Fianna Fáil as well as being a member of the National Executive. Born in Rooskey, he is married with a family of seven and resides at 'Mount Carmel' on the Dublin Road. Proprietor of the *Longford News*; Chairman and Managing Director of C&D Petfoods Ltd and Chairman and Director of ABC Finance Ltd are just some of his business interests. He was Director of Elections for Fianna Fáil in the last general election and is President of Longford Chamber of Commerce.'

In his election campaign Reynolds told the people of Longford that the future development of the county must lie in the creation of new jobs and in the ability of the area to attract new industry. He felt Longford's record of success was quite good but there was a danger of being too complacent.

Each week when he read of very large industries going to Wicklow, Clare and Mayo he asked the question: 'Are we resting on our laurels?'

When the votes were counted he received a staggering total of 906 first preferences and topped the poll. It was an impressive victory.

The *Leader* reported: 'The popularity of Albert was evident when crowds who had gathered at the Temperance Hall for hours beforehand cheered loudly when they heard the result.'

In an early morning interview he declared that in his memory it was the highest vote ever recorded at a County Council election in Longford. He admitted that he did not expect such a sweeping victory and added that he would concentrate on the living conditions of the poorer people. He also promised greater industrial retraining in the area, and to try to bring further employment to the county.

The new Councillor Reynolds took an interest in all local issues, including the army which has a barracks in Longford. During a special County Council meeting on housing in 1977 he suggested the army take over the old technical school to provide accommodation for 150 extra personnel.

At Council meetings Reynolds sat next to Frank Carter, the Fianna Fáil leader in the Chamber. Normally Councillors worked their way up the table over the years.

Then came the '77 election.

Longford/Westmeath had been rejoined as a single five-seater constituency in 1947, but was reduced to a four-seater in 1961 with part of Westmeath included in County Kildare. There were a number of minor changes subsequently until the constituency was again divided into Longford/Roscommon and Westmeath in 1992.

The constituency was the home of Fine Gael's General Seán MacEoin, known as the 'Blacksmith of Ballinalee' who had led an ambush against the Black and Tans, killing twenty of them, during the War of Independence. He was subsequently Chief of Staff of the new Free State and later served as Minister for Justice and Minister for Defence in the two coalition governments of the 1950s.

Fianna Fáil had taken two of the four seats since it became a four-seater in 1961. In 1965 there were several recounts before Paddy Lenihan (father of Brian Lenihan and Minister of State Mary O'Rourke) was declared elected for the party, and it was finally established that General Seán MacEoin had lost his seat.

The death of Paddy Lenihan led to a by-election on 14 April 1970, when Paddy Cooney was elected for Fine Gael. He was fewer than 1,000 votes ahead of the Fianna Fáil candidate, Seán Keegan.

In 1973 Fianna Fáil took a knock when, for the first time since the constituency had become a four-seater in 1961, Fianna Fáil won only one seat as against Fine Gael's two (Independent Joe Sheridan held the fourth). Fine Gael had managed this with 37 per cent of the first preference votes as against 38.4 per cent for Fianna Fáil. The successful Fianna Fáil TD was Frank Carter, with Seán Keegan and Seán Fallon (now Cathaoirleach of the Seanad) losing out.

Frank Carter was born in Ballinamore, Co Leitrim, in 1910. His father, Thomas Carter, had served as a Cumann na nGaedheal Deputy for Sligo/Leitrim in 1923 and later as a Fianna Fáil Deputy for Longford/Westmeath from 1943 to 1951. He had been one of a group of nine TDs who broke with Cumann na nGaedheal over WT Cosgrave's failure to honour undertakings given to the 'Army Mutineers' in 1924. The TDs formed the National Group and resigned *en bloc* from the Dáil in 1924. He subsequently joined Fianna Fáil.

His son Frank, who was manager of a footwear firm in Longford, was elected to the Dáil in 1951 and 1954, but was defeated in the '57 election by Ruadhri O'Bradaigh of Sinn Féin. He was re-elected in the elections of '61, '65, '69 and '73 when Fianna Fáil ended up with one seat. This situation caused major concern in the party within the constituency.

Furthermore, the Fine Gael/Labour Coalition had broken up and there was every chance that Fianna Fáil would increase its number of seats under Jack Lynch, and get back the second seat in Longford/Westmeath.

As the Fianna Fáil strategists got to work there was uproar at a meeting of the Comhairle Dáil Cheanntair in January 1977 when a motion was passed agreeing that a County Longford running mate for Frank Carter be selected. The *Longford Leader* speculated that Councillor Mickey Doherty (now constituency adviser to Albert Reynolds) would probably secure the nomination ahead of Councillor Reynolds and others.

Soon Frank Carter used the traditional ploy of saying he would not run again in order to drum up sympathy support.

'After I was elected to the Council Frank told me privately he wouldn't be going again,' said Reynolds. 'Later he said he definitely was going. In the end I had to decide to stand my ground or pull out.'

The Irish Times political correspondent, Denis Coughlan, saw the issue in rather more blunt, political terms. He wrote: 'When the ageing Mr Carter made the error of trawling for a sympathy vote by announcing that he might not run again, the young Albert was through the opening like a ferret after a rabbit.'

'It was certainly tough to go against the sitting TD whose father before had been the TD and where the tradition of Fianna Fáil had never been broken, where the outgoing TD had always been returned,' he told journalist Deirdre Purcell. 'But I was so far down the line, I'd even made management changes so that the business could carry on . . . I said, to hell, I decided to contest the Convention.'

The date of the Convention was set for Sunday, 22 May 1977, in the County Hall in Mullingar. The tension increased when the Fianna Fáil National Executive decided to field only one candidate from County Longford.

Previewing the event the *Longford Leader* described Albert Reynolds as the 'pin-up boy' who was likely to capture the support of the 'young bloods' at the Convention, while Frank Carter could rely on the old-timers.

The selection Convention was chaired by the party spokesman on Industry and Commerce, Des O'Malley, who warned the delegates that if Fianna Fáil did not win an extra seat in Longford/Westmeath, they would not win the election.

It took one and a half hours for all the delegates to be ratified before the Longford vote was taken. Three candidates were nominated, Councillor Michael McCarthy of Granard, Councillor Albert Reynolds and Deputy Frank Carter.

Years later Granard delegate, John Scanlon from Rathcronan, recalled how Frank Carter had been adamant at the beginning of the meeting that another Longford Town name should not be put forward.

'I pointed out that what was required was a younger man as the youth of the county didn't know Mr Carter. He raged and ranted and accused Councillor Michael McCarthy of prompting me, although nothing could be further from the truth . . . To make a long story short, my proposal was carried and the name of Mr Albert Reynolds was sent forward and duly ratified.'

Only one vote was needed. Reynolds secured a massive 209 votes from the 302 cumainn members representing the two counties. Councillor McCarthy secured just 12 votes while Frank Carter managed a mere 77 votes.

Carter immediately accused Des O'Malley of rigging the convention.

'He (Carter) cut the stones out of Mullingar that evening as he tore off after being beaten,' one delegate told the *Leader*.

In local folklore the night of the Convention is known as 'the night of the short knives', because Reynolds was standing so close to Frank Carter.

The voting then took place for the Westmeath candidates. Senators Seán Keegan and Seán Fallon were selected while a meeting of the Fianna Fáil National Executive later added Mullingar barrister Henry Abbot.

There was further controversy at the Convention, however, when three cumainn from Co Longford and one from Westmeath were not allowed to vote because they were not officially registered.

Later it emerged that a number of prominent Fianna Fáil people in the constituency had tried hard to persuade Frank Carter to step down, rather than be beaten, but to no avail.

Carter was beaten and humiliated because he had not seen the writing on the wall. Fianna Fáil was in a hungry mood, and wanted new, young blood. Albert Reynolds, with his background in business, ideally fitted the bill.

It was a sad day for Frank Carter. In an interview with the *Longford Leader* back in February 1975 he had said: 'My father had a great way with people. I don't think I have the same knack. A politician survives with the support of his people. I think I often lost ground by being too candid with people.'

Had he stepped down, as advised in the run-up to the Convention, glowing tributes would have been paid to him. But he chose to fight on and his career ended in a bitter defeat.

In an exclusive interview with the *Longford Leader* Frank Carter claimed Fianna Fáil was now a leaderless party and that he had been ditched because of his attitude to the North. No way was he backing Albert Reynolds in the election, and no way was he asking his supporters to do so. He claimed it was a conspiracy within Fianna Fáil at National Executive and Parliamentary Party level that got rid of him.

Albert Reynolds was philosophical about the departure of Frank Carter.

'Sure, there was sadness at Frank Carter's defeat because it was the end of an era, and you would be sorry to see anyone go,' he told the *Longford Leader*. 'But time and tide wait for no man. It's not alone in Longford that a sitting TD went, but in neighbouring Roscommon this also happened (Dr Hugh Gibbons). There was a mandate given to Jack Lynch to prepare a new team for this election.'

But for Albert Reynolds the nomination was the vital break he needed. Success in the election would mean a foothold in the Dáil, and who knew what might await him after that.

The 1977 election campaign brought back Albert Reynolds' former ballroom promotion skills into play. Old friends were called on to lend a hand. One of the first to volunteer his support was singer Larry Cunningham.

Albert's partner, the editor of the *Longford News*, Derek Cobbe, designed full colour posters, the first time ever a Dáil candidate had used them. Cobbe also came up with the election slogan: 'To get things done, vote Reynolds one'.

There were objections from Fianna Fáil to personal posters, so this problem was got round by printing that they were sponsored by Larry Cunningham. The Country 'n' Irish singer got fully immersed in the campaign and personally pasted the posters on poles and corrugated sheds from Finea to Lanesborough. An eight-page election newspaper was even specially produced.

Reynolds also had a pleasant easy manner with people.

'Unlike many other politicians Albert Reynolds is a fairly straightforward person,' wrote Eugene McGee, editor of the *Longford Leader*. 'What you see is what you get – almost. Outwardly he is most anxious to be classified as the "hail fellow, well met" type of individual so beloved of Irish people, as opposed to the more serious, academic type of person as personified by a Taoiseach like Garret FitzGerald, for instance. There are no airs and graces about Albert. He might have driven a £52,000 Jaguar, one of the few concessions he made to his enormous wealth, but he was also capable of stopping the Jaguar when he met a few County Council workers on the road and having a chat as if he was one of their next-door neighbours. As they would say in Longford: "He's not a bit uppity in himself at all." Lots of people will have a chat with you, but few of them manage to make it sincere. Albert does.'

Even Albert's name is an electoral advantage, McGee argued.

'It's a nice cosy name, conjuring up an image of a friendly farmer, a beaming bookie or a chattering comedian. Somehow "Paddy Reynolds" or "Charlie Reynolds" would not sound as homely as Albert. Have you noticed how often the man is referred to in the media as "Uncle Albert"?'

In 1977 Albert Reynolds was also able to ride on Fianna Fáil's rising tide. The party won major public support as the electorate rejected the Coalition's repressive policies and very strong anti-Republican line on the North as exemplified by Ministers Paddy Cooney and Conor Cruise O'Brien.

A hugely popular manifesto was produced which promised to create jobs and stem rising unemployment. Rates were to be abolished; so, too, was car tax.

It was an extravagant manifesto by any standards, and contained plans that would plunge the economy into serious trouble.

On the day the manifesto was launched the then Government Press Secretary, Frank Dunlop, met the Labour Parliamentary Secretary to the Minister for Health and Social Welfare, Frank Cluskey, on the corridors of Leinster House.

'Fuck ye,' said Cluskey. 'Ye're buying votes.' In later years Albert Reynolds claimed he hadn't read the manifesto until after the election.

'When I was asked my view on that manifesto, I said it was a crime to write it, and an even bigger crime to implement it,' he told journalist Deirdre Purcell. However, this was not the view Albert Reynolds gave during the election campaign.

In an interview with John Donlon, then a journalist with the *Longford Leader,* on 3 June 1977, he said:

'Our proposals are based on an expanding economy and better management of the resources available to us. We will be seeking more from the European Fund . . . our manifesto is well thought out and I find it appealing to the public. We have never come up with a policy manifesto before we could not deliver.'

Asked if there was a danger that he might misuse the *Longford News* to further his election campaign, he replied that he had equal publicity in the *Leader*.

'If a paper became really partisan, it would have very little future,' he declared.

Reporter Donlon then asked Reynolds about the charge by many of his opponents that he was a speculator. He replied:

'That charge is unjustified. If developing a business is speculation, then in my view I'm a speculator, but it's the wrong terminology for it.

I started at the bottom and came up the hard way. You hear about the fellow who makes it in America or England. Why shouldn't a local man who makes it at home be admired? I started earning £2.20 a week in Bórd Na Mona, and then I worked for CIE for £3.50 a week. Personally I don't think I've changed that much. I know the problems people face right up along the line. Unfortunately in Ireland, if you do well, people are inclined to knock you down.'

There was, also, in the '77 election, the thorny problem of the Independent candidate, Joe Sheridan, who was running for election again. Albert had, in the past, worked for Sheridan, who was still operating out of his old base in the Longford Arms Hotel. To add to the embarrassment, Albert's brother Jim was backing Sheridan.

Joe Sheridan says they were not really competing for the same votes.

'Albert was going after the Fianna Fáil vote, and I never got too many of those anyway. Sometimes when we were canvassing in a place like Longford we might see each other from a distance, but we would turn tail and avoid a meeting.'

Albert Reynolds, too, saw no problem, in public at any rate.

'Everyone is not enemies in politics,' he said. 'I happened to be running the hotel in 1961 when Joe Sheirdan came in to me there. He was after being ditched by Fine Gael and he was looking for a place to conduct his Independent campaign. We agreed to give him space in the hotel and he's been there since. I don't think anybody should fall out over politics. I don't read it as any personal animosity. There's room for us all.'

In his platform speeches Reynolds concentrated on what he personally had to offer Longford.

'I was talking about more factories and more jobs for young people, and I said that if I didn't deliver I wouldn't be back. Jack Lynch told me it was dangerous language.'

As election day drew near, Fianna Fáil's popularity increased. The party knew there was great antipathy towards the Coalition but were unable to quantify it.

Two days before voting *The Irish Times* conducted a poll which showed that Fianna Fáil would win a massive majority. However, it was not published because they did not believe the figures.

When the votes were counted, Fianna Fáil had swept to victory with eighty-four seats, the largest in the history of the State.

Down in Longford/Westmeath Joe Sheridan again headed the poll, but Fianna Fáil won the required two seats. Albert Reynolds polled 7,064 votes, a significant achievement for a first-time candidate. Seán Keegan was the other Fianna Fáil man elected, with Gerry L'Estrange taking a seat for Fine Gael. The vote had split well with Fianna Fáil taking out a Government Minister, Paddy Cooney.

Albert Reynolds headed for Dublin and Leinster House.

– 8 –

Headmaster of The Postmen

In the Coffee Dock in Jury's Hotel in Dublin a small group of Fianna Fáil politicians started to meet regularly in the spring of 1979. There was increasing dissatisfaction with the Fianna Fáil leadership and straw polls taken among the backbenchers showed that Charles Haughey was the one to help them keep their seats and lead them into the next election.

And so the gang of five came into being: Jackie Fahey, Tom McEllistrim, Seán Doherty, Mark Killilea and Albert Reynolds.

There was little doubt in the mind of anyone who knew Reynolds but that he would back Charles Haughey in any leadership contest.

The two had first met when the former Taoiseach, Seán Lemass, sent his son-in-law, Charles Haughey, on an organisational mission to Longford in the late 1950s.

Furthermore, Reynolds had been an almost daily visitor to the public gallery at the Four Courts during the Arms Trial in 1970.

From the time he had become a Dáil Deputy, Albert Reynolds had clearly shown that he was a man in a hurry.

His ability to make interesting economic speeches from the backbenches marked him out as someone worth cultivating by anyone seeking the leadership.

Albert Reynolds made his maiden speech to the Dáil on the Industrial Development Bill on 30 November 1977.

In his lengthy contribution he touched on themes he would return to again and again through his years as a Minister and front-bench spokesman.

He was critical of the IDA over its dependence on multi-national investers and its very cautious approach to new ventures.

'They will have to be a little more adventurous if we are to come to grips with this great national problem . . . History has made us a dependant race and we always look to someone else to solve our problems. Down the country they look to Dublin and to this House to solve the unemployment problem, and of late are starting to look to Brussels to solve our problems. Nobody will solve our problems for us. The world does not owe us a living.

'American banks back the man and the idea, and our banks back assets and securities. It is time to look after our own. If we look after the small man, the big man will look after himself . . . I believe there are many people who would put their money where their mouths are but they should be given a fair return on their investment.'

The former Summerhill scholar was also critical of the education system for being too academic:

'The future is in industry, not in office jobs . . . I started work as a penpusher during a recession and I was prepared to take whatever was available . . . There is nothing worse for young people than sitting around doing nothing. After a year of idleness they will have chips on their shoulders and will be easily lured into subversive organisations . . . they will rebel against society. Revolutions do not grow; they just happen.'

His success was seen in the June 1979 County Council elections when he romped home with 1,146 first preference votes.

At this time a key Haughey team consisting of PJ Mara and Haughey aide, Brendan O'Donnell, set up a detailed routine of getting to know deputies and helping them solve their problems. In the words of one politician, the main aim of Mara and O'Donnell was to 'find out where people itched so that Haughey could scratch'. Reynolds' easy manner made him a prime mover in winning friends for the Haughey camp.

Charles Haughey, then Minister for Health, made a point of calling on TDs and giving them good news to announce, relating to hospital extensions and the like, in their constituencies.

In October 1979 Haughey visited Longford himself and announced that a twenty-bed acute medical unit was to be set up at the Mater Nursing Home in Edgeworthstown. During his visit he lunched at the Reynolds' home, Mount Carmel, on the Dublin road.

But Albert Reynolds' exact role in preparing the ground for Haughey's leadership bid is disputed by those closely involved in it.

In an interview in the *Sunday Tribune* in February '92 Jackie Fahey claimed Albert Reynolds was a 'very active supporter of Charles Haughey, who used his easy style to sound out support'.

However, Tom McEllistrim said, 'Albert Reynolds never took any active part. He was not a central figure'. Mark Killilea agreed with Tom McEllistrim.

Albert Reynolds was certainly an admirer of Haughey's. Shortly after his appointment as Minister he told Vincent Kelly in the *Longford Leader*: 'I think Jack Lynch did a good job for the past thirteen years, but I believe a new style of leadership is needed to take us into the 1980s'. He claimed that the entire Longford Fianna Fáil organisation supported him in backing Haughey in the leadership stakes.

Reynolds had become cool with Lynch's leadership of the party. In 1979 he was put in charge of the European elections in Leinster and was given a dressing down for the poor performance.

Jack Lynch resigned voluntarily on 5 December 1979 following the loss of two by-elections in Cork. He was on a visit to the United States when he heard the news and gave journalists a strong indication that he would resign in January.

A further admission to the Washington Press Club that he had given permission for British overflights along the Border as part of a joint Government drive against terrorism caused a storm of controversy to erupt at home. Fianna Fáil Deputy, Bill Loughnane, accused Lynch of lying to the Dáil.

At a Parliamentary Party meeting on 10 November Haughey finally spoke in a rhetorical style, making reference to Pádraig Pearse.

The speech was circulated to the Irish party on a US Air Force plane heading south in the United States. Up in the front section it was discussed by the political editor of *The Irish Times*, Dick Walsh, and the RTE's Political Correspondent Seán Duignan, later Government Press Secretary to Albert Reynolds.

'You have to know the code,' said Duignan wisely, 'they're sending semaphore messages to each other across the Atlantic. The people in the back (Jack Lynch and his party) know what it means and they don't like it.'

When Lynch visited a ranch outside Houston, Texas, the next day, Dick Walsh wrote a piece saying the Taoiseach was meeting some real cowboys for a change.

Back in Dublin, Lynch told a Parliamentary Party meeting that he had heard of caucus meetings and he asked what was going on. Only P Flynn, now Ireland's EC Commissioner, stood up and publicly admitted his role. Later Lynch said Flynn was the only one of the conspirators he could have any respect for because he at least stood up to be counted.

Haughey meanwhile totted up his numbers and concluded he would have fifty-eight votes to Colley's twenty-four.

Seán Doherty, who was present, laughed at the sum.

'Do you know, Charlie, you're the worst fucking judge of people I ever met,' he declared.

On the morning Jack Lynch quit, Albert Reynolds and his wife, Kathleen, were about to board a plane at Dublin Airport for a holiday in the sun. Suddenly there was a paging call for him in the departure lounge. It was Ray MacSharry with the news that Lynch had finally quit. Albert and Kathleen cancelled their plans and returned to Jury's Hotel where he spent two days and nights sounding out support for Haughey.

Electioneering continued for forty-eight hours. Albert Reynolds spent almost the entire time on his feet canvassing for Haughey.

'In the space of one twenty-minute period there were eighteen calls for me at the hotel,' he said.

His wife, Kathleen, took many of the calls. One group rang from Kerry and wanted to talk to Albert about his allegiances.

'They were in a pub somewhere in Kerry and said they would stay there until Albert rang them,' she said.

One of Reynolds' most satisfying moments was in gaining a last minute vote for Haughey.

'There was a particular deputy I was trying to contact and I couldn't,' he said. 'He had disappeared for fourteen hours and was obviously in the Colley camp. The next I saw of him was when I walked into the room where the election was being held. I just looked at him and knew we were going to get his vote.'

Haughey, however, wanted a member of the Cabinet to propose him, and was disappointed when Brian Lenihan declined. Major Vivian de Valera also refused, but George Colley was taken aback when Ray MacSharry, a Junior Minister in his own Department, and later Ireland's EC Commissioner, agreed.

There was a final blow for the Colley camp when Michael O'Kennedy announced his support for Haughey.

In his book *The Party, Inside Fianna Fáil* Dick Walsh quotes Des O'Malley who, long afterwards, watching O'Kennedy's European Commission limousine passing by, muttered 'Judas's chariot'.

In the subsequent leadership vote count MacSharry was the teller for the Haughey camp. The plan was that if they were successful, MacSharry would turn towards them and raise his right hand. In the crush that followed he had difficulty raising his hand, but managed to get it as far as his face. Haughey had won the day by forty-four votes to thirty-eight.

Haughey's election as Taoiseach caused an outpouring of invective against him in the Dáil by the Opposition. Fine Gael leader Garret

FitzGerald referred to what he called Haughey's 'flawed pedigree'. Labour leader Frank Cluskey said Haughey's ambition was to own Ireland, while Noel Browne compared him to the Portuguese dictator, Antonio Salazar.

Meanwhile, the Haughey camp within Fianna Fáil were ecstatic. Three of the existing Fianna Fáil Ministers were dropped – Jim Gibbons, Bobby Molloy and Martin O'Donoghue whose Department of Economic Planning and Development was dissolved.

Albert Reynolds had no idea of Haughey's Cabinet plans. At 8.00 am on Tuesday 11 December, he got a call from Haughey's private secretary, Catherine Butler, who told him that the new Taoiseach-elect had been trying to contact him over the weekend. She told him to go directly to the party leader's office when he got to Leinster House that morning.

When he arrived at Leinster House he was met by Ms Butler who brought him to Haughey's office herself.

Once inside the door Haughey's first words to Reynolds were, 'I have a right bastard of a job for you – Transport and Posts & Telegraphs. Do you want it?'

Reynolds thought the job was just a junior ministry and accepted. Suddenly it dawned on him that this was a full Cabinet post. His first reaction was to ring Kathleen, but he couldn't because the phone was dialling engaged. He gave his friend, Noel Hanlon, his measurements and sent him across to Grafton Street for a new suit. Noel selected a grey and brown check suit. He matched it with a gleaming white shirt, striped tie and brown shoes.

In Longford the line was still ringing engaged. Technicians were called to find out why the phone wasn't working. In the end it turned out that an upstairs extension had been left off the hook.

Later, Noel Hanlon got through to Kathleen to tell her she was a Minister's wife. Hanlon's employee, Christy Kelly, drove her and the four children attending Longford schools to Leinster House in Albert's old white Mercedes. Albert had travelled up to Dublin earlier in the day in Hanlon's car with Councillor Mickey Doherty. A black State Mercedes was waiting to bring him home.

Christy Kelly then picked up sixteen year-old Miriam and twelve year-old Emer from their school in Banagher and took them to Dublin.

He had another run to Roscrea to pick up fourteen year-old Philip who was studying for his Intermediate Certificate at the Cistercian College there.

In school, Albert's youngest daughter, Andrea, then aged seven, was asked by her schoolmates what her father did.

'He's become headmaster of the postmen,' she replied.

Since their father was also to be responsible for radio and television, newspapers were curious to know if Albert had any favourite programmes at the time.

Mainly current affairs programmes like *Frontline*, and of course the *News*, older daughter Miriam said, and he liked to watch the *Late Late Show* and *Match of the Day* on Saturday nights.

The Reynolds' five daughters and two sons made no secret of their preferences. They included *Grandstand*, *Grange Hill* and *Little House on the Prairie*. And, of course *Charlie's Angels*.

The entire family was delighted, but there were still no plans to leave their Longford base and move to Dublin.

'I wouldn't have been sore if I didn't get a Cabinet post,' Albert Reynolds said later. 'I didn't expect to get one, and I didn't go looking for one. The evening before the posts were announced I was down in Clara buying bones for C&D.'

But the portfolio he was given was a generous recognition by Charles Haughey of the role Albert Reynolds had played in his leadership bid.

Albert Reynolds was the second deputy from Longford/Westmeath to be given Post & Telegraphs. In 1951, Erskine Childers, later to become President, held the ministry.

In Longford the mood was exuberant.

'Albert's Big Day' screamed a banner headline in the *Longford Leader*. The front page carried a picture of the new Minister flanked by the Taoiseach and two other first-time Ministers, Maire Geoghegan-Quinn (Gaeltacht) and Ray MacSharry (Agriculture).

In the lead story, reporter Anne Sweeney speculated that Councillor Mickey Doherty might be given a place on the RTE Authority which came under Albert's charge.

The *Leader* reckoned that a few Longford people must be on the top priority list for new telephones.

Albert's only sister, Teresa, who was living with her husband Charlie Reynolds, in Tooman, Bornacoola, had no telephone. She was expected to give her brother a ring.

'He was always a hard goer and a hard worker, but I never thought he would go this far,' she said. 'We only heard last night when the newsflash came on the television, but we were delighted to hear of his success.'

Albert's older brother, Joe, predicted that he would never leave Longford.

'He's too cemented there. He is very interested in the locals, and I don't see him losing contact with his constituents because he is now a Minister,' he said.

One of Albert's biggest fans, his old primary school teacher, Elizabeth McLoughlin, had been trying to get a phone installed for six years. When she heard of Albert's appointment on 11 December, she reckoned she would have it by Christmas Day.

'If he can't get it done, who can?' she laughed.

Elizabeth then went on to make a prediction.

'I always expected that he would get on like a house on fire. He's very progressive and I expect that he will be the next Taoiseach after Haughey, and will eventually end up in Áras an Uachtaráin.' So far Elizabeth McLoughlin has been right.

On Saturday 15 December 1979 Albert Reynolds was given the first of many triumphant welcomes to Longford when the local pipe band led a torchlight procession into the town to a bumper banquet at the Sunset Club.

As new Minister for Transport and Power, and Posts and Telegraphs, Albert Reynolds had responsibility for more than 50,000 people in CIE, P&T, Irish Shipping and RTE.

He had a look at his portfolio, saw that RTE was run by professionals, and decided to leave well enough alone for the time being.

A bitter nineteen week old postal strike had just ended, and Albert decided to visit the workers, having first briefed himself on the issues. It was the first strike for decades.

'I realised there must be something very seriously wrong,' he said. He headed for the Sheriff Street sorting office.

'The place was a hive. I stood talking to a couple of guys at a long bench and a cold sharp breeze struck me right across the face.'

The Minister searched around until he found the source of the breeze. A window had been broken for three months.

'Why don't you fix it?' he asked the supervisor.

'You don't understand, Minister . . .,' said the supervisor.

'No, I don't. You tell me. The boys are here sorting letters, but it would be warmer outside on a picket.'

'It's not my fault,' pleaded the supervisor.

'Well, there are five or six small glaziers around Amiens Street. In the morning go down there, order the glass and get them to fix it,' said the Minister.

'I can't do that, Minister.'

'For Heaven's sake, why not?'

'I've no authority. It's the Board of Works who do that.'

'Go down to Amiens Street. I'll go back to my office in the GPO. I'll find out what the system is and, if necessary, I'll pay for it.'

'You don't understand, Minister . . . If the Board of Works come here and find that window fixed, they'll take their craftsmen out and they'll bring ours out in sympathy. You'll have a strike on your hands.'

(Pause)

'Well, here's what you do. Go down to Amiens Street, get the window fixed and send me the bill. When the Board of Works ring you up to say they're coming to fix the window, break it, and let them put in another pane.'

Reynolds believed in treating people well. His philosophy was that if the civil servants were happy at their work, then productivity increased. An unhappy civil service was good for no-one.

One morning, having been in office for only a short time, Minister Reynolds left the GPO on O'Connell Street in a hurry to get to Government Buildings. His driver was nowhere in sight.

So Albert approached the first driver in a line of post vans.

'Would you ever drop me over to Government Buildings?' he enquired of the startled driver.

'Ah, maybe you'd prefer the van behind me,' he replied.

'Why?' asked Albert.

'I've no seat for a passenger,' said the driver.

'Arragh, pull up that big bag there, man. Sure won't it do me grand,' said Albert.

The new Minister adopted a friendly attitude to all his civil servants working on the principle that if there was a problem he'd hear about it in good time from some source or other.

Once, at an internal function, he asked a staff member what he could do best, and was told he would have to restore the credibility of the Department with the public.

'We're fed up watching people smile when we say we work for the P&T,' said the staffer. 'Give us back a pride in our jobs, and you'll have succeeded where nobody else could.'

117

Albert also empathised with the frustration felt by the average Dublin bus driver.

'He has to contend with traffic chaos, bad buses and abuse from the public. How must he feel? Put yourself in the guy's position.'

But Reynolds' real success in his first ministry was in transforming the Irish telephone system.

'When I used to lift a telephone before becoming Minister, I always assumed that the staff were out having coffee,' he told John Kelly of the *Sunday Press*. 'It's only now I realise what they had to put up with. The public just does not understand. We didn't have to revamp existing systems. By starting from behind, we could be first.'

It galled Albert Reynolds to think that there were thousands of people around the country who were more than willing to pay for telephones, but couldn't get them. He was determined to update the creaking system.

'I look at the whole thing as a businessman's dream,' he said. 'Here you have more than 100,000 customers, looking for equipment, and you have to turn them away, although they're at your door with money in their hands. It's a dream. Where else would you get a business like that? And how many have not even applied yet?'

In 1980 an irate member of the public, who couldn't get his telephone repaired, wrote to the *Evening Herald* lambasting the Minister for incompetence. Albert tracked the person down.

When the letter-writer received a call from the Minister at his work-place, he didn't believe it.

'Hello, who's that?' said the letter-writer.

'It's Albert Reynolds, I'd like to talk to you about your . . . '

'Would you ever fuck off, and stop messing,' said the letter-writer.

Eventually, Albert convinced the man of his identity. A P&T crew arrived that evening and the line was repaired.

Reynolds succeeded in securing the necessary capital for his Department and set about the task, drawing on his business skills.

Before he left office in 1981 he had prepared the groundwork for the transformation of the telephone system, the benefits of which are still being reaped.

During this time Albert Reynolds always maintained excellent relations with the press.

His basic view – which would change later when he became Taoiseach – was the old Hollywood maxim, 'Don't read your publicity, weigh it'.

Never slow to announce progress in areas such as new phones, a local £1,000,000 Telecom Éireann engineering headquarters near his Longford home, which he opened himself on 9 February 1981, was quickly christened 'The Albert Memorial'.

In one celebrated interview on the *Mike Murphy Show* on RTE television he even donned stetson and cowboy gear to sing the old Jim Reeves' composition *Put Your Sweet Lips a Little Closer to the Phone.*

Nor was the Minister with responsibility for broadcasting embarrassed at a reception in Dublin Castle for musicians and singers during the Eurovision Song Contest, when it was learned that the catering company was from Longford. Half of those present appeared to be from Longford. It was Albert's way of giving the local people a big day out in Dublin.

Meanwhile, Charles Haughey was heading a Cabinet in which personal relations were not good. There was a clear coolness with Des O'Malley and George Colley.

Albert Reynolds had strongly favoured the side-lining of George Colley after the '79 leadership battle.

When Haughey contacted Reynolds by telephone following a controversial speech by Colley in Baldoyle on 21 December 1980, Reynolds asked of Colley: 'Is he still there?'

Haughey, who had major reservations about the '77 manifesto, was expected to tackle the nation's critical debt. But having identified the problem, he proceeded to do the opposite. Public pay soared and plans to widen the tax net were shelved in the face of opposition.

Many of Haughey's actions were aimed at obtaining an overall majority for himself in his first election as leader of Fianna Fáil. Victory in a by-election in Donegal South-West in 1981 gave him a boost and he planned to have the general election in the spring of that year. However, Haughey's plans were delayed by the Stardust tragedy when forty-eight young people were burned to death in his own constituency on St Valentine's night.

Then came the H-Block hunger strike campaign. Haughey finally dissolved the Dáil and called an election for 11 June.

Despite favourable opinion polls early in the campaign, Fianna Fáil slipped badly in the closing days and ended up with its poorest showing for twenty years. With only seventy-eight seats Fianna Fáil went into Opposition and a minority Coalition of Fine Gael and Labour took over. For their survival they depended on a few Independent deputies.

Down in Longford Albert Reynolds had little to fear heading into the election.

Speaking at the opening of Mayfair Fashions in Glack in February, three months before polling day, he was able to point out that the results achieved under the IDA's Small Industries Programme in the county were double the national average. Over the previous three years manufacturing employment had risen by almost 33 per cent.

With Independent Joe Sheridan finally deciding to stand down, the outcome of the election in Longford/Westmeath was a foregone conclusion – Fianna Fáil and Fine Gael should win two seats each.

Former Minister, Paddy Cooney, who had lost his seat in 1977 was determined to regain it, and did so.

In Fianna Fáil Albert Reynolds was a certainty. He topped the poll with 10,450 first preference votes, well in excess of the quota.

The only issue was whether the second outgoing Fianna Fáil Deputy, Seán Keegan, could be pushed out by Seán Fallon of Athlone. In the end Fallon was narrowly defeated by 483 votes on the eighth and final count.

Significantly, however, Martin Hurson, a H-Block candidate, who died on hunger strike, polled over half a quota, showing there was still a strong base of Republican support in the constituency which had in the past elected Sinn Féin President Ruairi O Bradaigh.

Now in Opposition, Albert Reynolds returned to his petfood business which was experiencing severe teething problems in getting off the ground.

– 9 –
The Battle For Tang Church

January 27 1982, is a day Charlie McCreevy will never forget. He had quickly become disillusioned with the economic policies pursued by Charles Haughey after he was elected Taoiseach. He made his views known in an interview in the *Sunday Tribune* and subsequently lost the Fianna Fáil party whip on 20 January 1982. After the vote to expel him, Haughey sent his State car to McCreevy's home in Sallins asking the rebel TD to get in touch with him. Not to be outdone, McCreevy sent a Mercedes and driver back to Kinsealy in North Dublin with the reply.

The Dáil resumed on 27 January but collapsed on a Budget vote. It was the only day that McCreevy sat in the Independent Dáil benches. A general election was called and McCreevy was automatically nominated for Kildare, thereby by-passing the normal procedure of having to reapply for the party whip.

Fianna Fáil knew it had difficulty with Haughey's appeal to some of the public, and his picture was dropped from much of the election literature. Albert Reynolds was appointed National Director of Elections.

The party tried to counter the criticism of its leader with accusations of a personal vendetta against Haughey.

In their book *The Boss*, Joe Joyce and Peter Murtagh point out that 'one of the more extraordinary charges was the claim by Albert Reynolds that Fine Gael had orchestrated a "whispering campaign" against Haughey in pubs.'

According to Reynolds, Garret FitzGerald had launched a personal, vindictive attack on Haughey from the day of his election as Taoiseach.

Could any journalist, he asked rhetorically at a press conference, point to a single fault in Haughey's handling of any issue?

As counting proceeded on Friday, 19 February, it became clear that no party would emerge with an overall majority.

But anti-Haugheyites had done well. Jim Gibbons returned in Carlow/Kilkenny as did Joe Walsh in Cork South-West at the expense of Flor Crowley, a sworn Haughey man. In Kildare where Charlie McCreevy had lost the party whip, he topped the poll with an astonishing 11,500 votes.

Down in Longford/Westmeath there were no surprises when Albert Reynolds topped the poll with 10,214 votes.

The four-seater again divided evenly between the two outgoing Fianna Fáil and Fine Gael deputies.

A significant arrival on the Fianna Fáil ticket this time, however, was Mary O'Rourke, a sister of Brian Lenihan, later appointed to the Cabinet by Charles Haughey, and who would go on to contest the party leadership against Albert Reynolds in 1992.

She defeated Seán Fallon for the party nomination in Westmeath and won a handsome 5,688 first preference votes, only losing out to her running mate, Seán Keegan, on the sixth count. An extra 7 per cent would have seen Fianna Fáil take a third seat. This is believed to have been the only occasion when Albert Reynolds deserted his good friend, Seán Fallon.

In 1981 Martin Hurson, the H-Block hunger-striker, had polled well, but this time the Sinn Féin candidate, Seán Lynch, did poorly. He became the first person to take the Government to court challenging their arbitrary powers under Section 31 of the *Broadcasting Act.* Constituency Minister Paddy Cooney, when in office, had taken the dramatic step of banning party political broadcasts by Sinn Féin.

Around this time, as rumours of a new coup against Haughey continued, there was speculation that events within Fianna Fáil could have an important bearing on the political future of Albert Reynolds.

The *Longford Leader* reported that the ongoing problems for Haughey could also provide headaches for Reynolds. If he remained loyal to Haughey, he was sure of a Cabinet seat provided Haughey formed the Government.

There had been a reported cooling of relations between himself and Haughey over the previous few months. But Albert Reynolds denied any such coolness or any change in his level of support for Haughey whom he expected to be the new Taoiseach. In fact Reynolds went on to become one of Haughey's chief handlers in the subsequent heave.

Haughey decided to tackle the leadership issue head-on and brought forward a meeting of the Parliamentary Party. His leading opponents, George Colley and Des O'Malley, met to consider strategy. Reluctantly Colley agreed to back O'Malley.

Although quite young, O'Malley had proved a tough and efficient Minister for Justice during the difficult period of the Arms Trial and its aftermath.

As the meeting of the Parliamentary Party drew nearer, the O'Malley camp felt confident of victory. With twenty-four hours to go, journalist Stephen Collins asked Haughey if he was going to resign.

'Would you fuck off,' Haughey roared at the frightened Collins. 'That's F-U-C-K, O-F-F,' he shouted, spelling out each letter.

Recovered from the trauma, Collins met a less fiery Albert Reynolds on his way out of Leinster House, who predicted that Haughey would easily win the leadership race.

'Who else will be able to do a deal with Gregory and the Workers' Party?' he asked.

During the heave, Martin O'Donoghue, one of the dissidents, met Albert Reynolds in his Ballsbridge apartment. O'Donoghue suggested to Reynolds that senior people should agree a replacement and then go to Haughey. Reynolds replied that there was no chance of success.

When O'Malley finally decided to contest the leadership late one night, Reynolds telephoned the *Irish Independent* to alert them to the statement and gave them plenty of counter quotes to lessen the damage.

Later Reynolds crossed the road from his Ballsbridge apartment to Jury's Hotel where he met other Haughey supporters, including Seán Doherty. From there, acting as a sort of *ad hoc* press officer for the Haughey camp, he telephoned the *Irish Press, The Irish Times* and *Cork Examiner*, continuing to be available into the small hours of the following morning, the day of the Parliamentary Party meeting itself.

That morning Fianna Fáil TDs and senators gathered in the Dáil's self-service restaurant. Reynolds sat inside the door alongside Ray MacSharry, Pádraig Flynn and Jim Tunney. When Martin O'Donoghue arrived, he was met with a glaring stare from Reynolds.

In the end, when the meeting took place, O'Malley withdrew following a request from Martin O'Donoghue.

Reynolds sat close to an ebullient Haughey at an impromptu press conference, with Ray MacSharry on the other side. Haughey promised stable government for five years.

Haughey quickly did a deal with the Workers' Party and Independent TD Tony Gregory, and was back in power.

As in February 1981, the key figures in the Cabinet were the old Haughey campaigners, including Albert Reynolds, who this time was appointed Minister for Industry and Energy. Seán Doherty was given the highly sensitive Justice portfolio.

Reynolds' promotion to the important portfolio of Industry and Energy was a clear sign of his ability, and a reward for the success he had achieved in his previous ministry between '79 and '81.

Along with another Haughey supporter, Ray McSharry, who was now Minister for Finance, he was to be responsible for the all-important job creation drive and industrial relations in the new Government.

The new Government took over the reins of power enthusiastically, with Ray MacSharry proclaiming 'boom and bloom' in contrast to the Coalition's message of 'doom and gloom'.

However, the Government was quickly beset by a number of bizarre events, characterised by Conor Cruise O'Brien as 'GUBU,' when he coined a notable phrase uttered by Haughey himself – grotesque, unprecedented, bizarre and unbelievable – in relation to the discovery of a wanted murder suspect Malcolm McArthur in the home of the then Attorney General, Patrick Connolly.

The strange events included the offering of the position of EC Commissioner to a Fine Gael Deputy, Richard Burke, and Fianna Fáil's subsequent failure to win the by-election in Dublin West; the death of a Fianna Fáil deputy, John Callanan, in Galway East at a critical time for Dáil numbers; and the revelation that Haughey had installed in the Dáil telephone equipment technically capable of over-riding other calls.

Reynolds had first sounded out Dick Burke as to whether he might be interested in the job of EC Commissioner. On their way into Leinster House Reynolds mentioned to the Fine Gael deputy that the Brussels job would have to be filled.

'You went the full term in your time,' Reynolds mused. 'Don't suppose you would be interested in going back?' Burke didn't say no, and eventually secured the job, much to Fine Gael's displeasure.

The Government's decision to remain neutral in the Falklands War did not make life any easier for the Industry Minister Albert Reynolds who was trying to encourage investment in Ireland.

In May '82 he told the *Sunday Independent* that while 'business tends to transcend all political barriers' he had met at least one disgusted industrialist on a trade mission in Britain.

Asked how he was enjoying his job, he replied: 'It is a heavy portfolio – I have twenty State companies for example – but I enjoy hard work. I wouldn't mind a bit of help though, perhaps a Minister of State. But that is up to the Taoiseach.'

And he had lots of advice for the business sector:

'The responsibility for viability and stability in a company rests in the first instance with management. The Government can do so much – but it can't solve everyone's problem.

'We need better communication between work-force and management . . . I want to see us getting further away from a "Them and Us" situation. Inefficiency must be rooted out and management must relate themselves more to what the customer wants.'

In an era of very high inflation Minister Reynolds kept emphasising that sacrifices would have to be made by having realistic wage levels.

His brief also included Energy and the difficulties associated with the Tara/Bula mining debacle, still unresolved twelve years later.

In office Reynolds had to contend with a number of controversies including the closure of the Ardmore Studios, Fieldcrest and the Clondalkin Paper Mills. He clearly marked himself off from politicians who loved setting up new State bodies when he disbanded three of them in one week – Ardmore Studios, Avoca Mines and Minera Teo.

But he counteracted this by capitalising to the full on the publicity surrounding the completion of the natural gas pipeline.

When it emerged in 1993 that Des O'Malley, as Minister for Industry and Energy in 1981, had received some financial contributions at election time from his brother-in-law, who was a director of Tara Mines, Reynolds was quizzed as to whether he received any money.

'I was Minister for Energy for a short period in 1982,' he replied. 'I do not have records for around that period and my personal recollection would not be perfect.'

The GUBU events of the summer of 1982 forced Haughey's enemies to think again about removing him as leader of the party. The Government was under increasing pressure from all sides. Ministers began to blame each other for various happenings.

Albert Reynolds, Minister for Energy, blamed Des O'Malley, Minister for Trade, Commerce and Tourism, for the price of petrol, double the level Reynolds had said it would be.

'I have responsibility for Whitegate – but I don't have responsibility for prices,' he declared.

An article in *Aspect* magazine in September '82 speculated that Albert Reynolds could be a compromise leader of Fianna Fáil, capable of uniting both camps.

'Behind the bluff bonhomie and easygoing demeanour there lurks in Albert Reynolds a keen ambition and an opportunistic sense that made him a millionaire in his private capacity' said the article. 'Translated into political life, that business acumen has led him, despite his public espousal of the Haughey faction, to leave lines of communication open into the other camp . . . There is no doubt that Reynolds considers himself a serious contender in the power struggle and there is a possibility that he could emerge as the man to bridge the gap if he can get over his image problem.'

On Friday, 1 October, old Haughey adversary, Charlie McCreevy, put down a motion of no confidence in him. Des O'Malley, who was on holiday in Spain, had to rush home, resign his seat in Cabinet – as did Martin O'Donoghue – before joining in the campaign.

Reynolds, MacSharry, Flynn and Doherty were again the leading handlers in the Haughey camp.

In his book *The Party* Dick Walsh wrote that not all messages delivered to deputies were simple enquiries:

'In one case, a racehorse trainer who was a substantial contributor to party funds made the call; in another, it was a hotel owner in a southern town; a third call was made by a businessman who had dealings with a deputy engaged in the manufacturing industry.'

But this time the dissidents were more determined and were insisting on pushing the issue to a vote. In the end Haughey won by an impressive fifty-eight votes to twenty-two. Outside Leinster House

Haughey supporters yelled 'bastard' and 'blueshirt' at Charlie McCreevy, and the Club of 22 was born.

Charles Haughey had survived again, but his victory was short-lived. Throughout the closing months of '82 there were questions asked about the running of the Garda Síochána under Justice Minister, Seán Doherty.

There was the Dowra affair, which involved a witness from Northern Ireland being held by the RUC so that he could not give evidence against a brother-in-law of the Minister, and the Tully affair in Roscommon where a Sergeant Tully of Boyle, Co Roscommon, had successfully resisted an attempt, in which the Minister was involved, to have him transferred.

The death of County Clare Deputy Dr Bill Loughnane and the hospitalisation of Jim Gibbons after a severe heart attack made the Government's position precarious.

Finally Fianna Fáil lost a motion of no confidence, and an election was called for 24 November. Exhausted deputies braced themselves for the third general election in eighteen months.

The November '82 election was a tame affair with little difference between Fianna Fáil and Fine Gael on the economic crisis. The issue of Haughey's credibility largely dominated the campaign.

This time Fianna Fáil was decisively beaten, returning to Leinster House with just seventy-five seats, down six in a mere eight months.

In Longford/Westmeath Albert Reynolds' vote dropped to 8,899 but he still topped the poll to be elected on the first count.

But a new figure, Mary O'Rourke, was on the march again. She had replaced Seán Fallon in the February election and had performed well, going on to be elected Senator. This time the competition between herself and the outgoing deputy, Seán Keegan, was intense.

O'Rourke told the electorate that members of Fine Gael had 'the stamp of the English men on them,' while Seán Keegan proclaimed that 'there are more atheists in the opposition parties than in any government in the world.'

O'Rourke's followers were said to have canvassed beyond Moate on the eastern side of the constituency, the area reserved for Keegan. Later he complained: 'I stayed in my own area. If I had travelled into Longford I might have got in. The message is that you have to be selfish.'

On the sixth count O'Rourke won the fourth and final seat from Keegan by a margin of just twenty-seven votes. Paddy Cooney and Gerry L'Estrange were returned as before for Fine Gael.

With just seventy-five seats Fianna Fáil was back in opposition and Albert Reynolds became Spokesman on Industry. He also resumed an active interest in C&D Foods, although in 1994 he insisted it had been purely in a non-executive director capacity.

On the national scene there was more trouble for Charles Haughey when the new Justice Minister, Michael Noonan, revealed that his predecessor, Seán Doherty, had initiated taps on the phones of two political journalists, Geraldine Kennedy and Bruce Arnold.

It also emerged that Seán Doherty had supplied Ray MacSharry with telephone recording equipment to bug a conversation he had with Martin O'Donoghue about MacSharry's financial affairs.

It was rumoured that £100,000 was on offer to MacSharry to change sides, and that Doherty could have £50,000 if he ditched Haughey. In their book *The Boss* Joe Joyce and Peter Murtagh recall how Albert Reynolds suggested to Martin O'Donoghue that he should talk to Ray MacSharry. When Reynolds gave O'Donogue's message to MacSharry, he was furious.

'I nearly hit the roof when I heard my name mentioned in connection with money,' said MacSharry. O'Donoghue denied there was any money on offer.

Within days the Garda Commissioner and Assistant Commissioner had resigned, MacSharry and Doherty had quit the Fianna Fáil front-bench and an internal party inquiry was underway into the whole affair. Those interviewed by the Tunney Inquiry included Ray MacSharry, Martin O'Donoghue, Albert Reynolds, Pádraig Flynn and Charles Haughey. Their report exonerated Haughey except for a minority report from committee member David Andrews who stated that 'on the principle of ultimate responsibility, he should have been so aware'.

But rumours were again rife that Haughey was on the brink of resignation, with the *Irish Press* carrying a detailed profile of Haughey's political career.

Charlie McCreevy said Fianna Fáil had now been reduced to a 'self-centred, advance-seeking cabal of opportunists' who had no interest in the Irish nation.

The Fianna Fáil Parliamentary Party met on Wednesday, 2 February, but the chairman, Jim Tunney, adjourned it immediately because of the death of Donegal TD Clem Coughlan on his way to Dublin.

The delay gave Haughey vital breathing space. Again the old team went to work on the telephones with Haughey insisting he would fight on. He was appalled at the continuing negative newspaper coverage.

'How do I stop this sewage coming out?' he asked PJ Mara in desperation. 'Is there any God up there?'

A motion demanding his resignation was put down by Dublin South Central Deputy, Ben Briscoe. The pressure on the TDs became obvious. A number collapsed, a few were hospitalised.

Already an unofficial leadership campaign was underway. North Tipperary Deputy Michael O'Kennedy was first off with his campaign being managed by his South Tipp colleague, Dr Seán McCarthy. Gerry Collins joined in from his hospital bed in the Mater.

But when the votes were counted Haughey had again survived, this time by forty votes to thirty-three.

Back in Opposition, Albert Reynolds gave a very colourful reaction to the Fine Gael-Labour Government's economic plan:

'In Iveagh House this document (Building on Reality) was launched at a lavish party attended by trade unionists, business people and every name one could think of – including men with six inch Havana cigars – and glasses of brandy. That was a nice sight for the people sitting at home who had no money to pay their bills on Friday, the people who are unemployed with no hope of a job . . .

'At Iveagh House as the Taoiseach was walking to the podium to announce the plan, a civil servant was whistling "Nearer My God to Thee", the air that was played by the band when the *Titanic* sank.'

The early years of the new Fine Gael/Labour Coalition were dominated to a large extent by the New Ireland Forum followed by the Anglo-Irish Agreement in 1985.

Excluding the former Fianna Fáil Ministers who subsequently left to form the Progressive Democrats, Albert Reynolds was the only Fianna Fáil frontbencher to publicly support the Agreement.

While he rarely spoke publicly on the North, his support was an early indication of his readiness for compromise and his anxiety for a push forward on an initiative.

Ever the pragmatist, he saw it as offering the best hope of civilised relations between the British and Irish Governments. His Cabinet colleagues embraced it belatedly when Fianna Fáil returned to power in 1987.

During his time as Opposition spokesman, Reynolds was highly critical of the handling of the affairs of Dublin Gas (Frank Cluskey resigned from the Coalition Cabinet over the affair) and also of the terms for issuing licences for oil exploration off the coast, frequently accusing the Government of mismanagement.

Meanwhile the expulsion of Des O'Malley from Fianna Fáil in February 1985 had strengthened Charles Haughey's grip on the party, and it only seemed a matter of time before he would return to power again.

The Coalition finally broke up on 20 January 1987 when Labour would not agree to Fine Gael's proposed Budget.

But despite Fianna Fáil's best ever election campaign, the achievement of a majority Government again eluded Haughey, who ended up with eighty-one seats, two short of an overall majority.

In Longford/Westmeath the retirement of Fine Gael's Gerry L'Estrange created an opportunity for Fianna Fáil to try for three out of the four seats. But it would take very careful campaign strategy.

Barrister Henry Abbot from Mullingar, who was not added to the 1982 party ticket against the wishes of the local organisation, now got another chance. Ideally situated in Mullingar, his location dovetailed with Mary O'Rourke in Athlone and Albert Reynolds in Longford.

The Director of Elections was Councillor Mickey Doherty.

'If we're going for three out of four seats, and we are, then the North Westmeath people will have to vote for the North Westmeath candidate (Abbot), the South Westmeath people will have to vote for the South Westmeath candidate (O'Rourke), and Longford people must vote entirely for the Longford candidate (Reynolds),' Doherty warned party supporters. 'We will only fail if somebody messes up.'

This time Albert Reynolds had only one third of the electorate in his area, and he left nothing to chance.

When his campaign team were advised that the occasional accompanying posters of Charles Haughey might not be helping his chances very much, they became even more occasional. In the run-up to voting Haughey told party headquarters that he would not be able to participate in the national campaign. 'I will not generally be available for television or radio appearances,' he said.

The *Longford Leader* reported that all seven members of the Reynolds family were on the canvass trail in Co Longford.

'Candidate Albert was joined early in the campaign by his nineteen year-old daughter, Emer, who is spending three days a week in North Longford. On her first day Emer canvassed over 170 votes in the Drumlish electoral area.'

Tension between the Fianna Fáil candidates was at a high, with Reynolds and O'Rourke engaging in what is now known in local folklore as 'the battle for Tang church'.

Part of the election campaign was after-Mass meetings throughout the constituency. The procedure was simple – the Director of Elections drew up a programme for the candidate to go to the churches in his/her local area.

The first stop on one such Sunday morning trip was Castledaly, and then on to Tang.

Tang is a small, rural village on the Longford/Westmeath border, and was assigned to the Westmeath candidate, Mary O'Rourke.

The chat between the political supporters was light-hearted until suddenly Seamus Browne, one of O'Rourke's henchmen, was overheard shouting: 'Holy fuck, look who has arrived'.

Having parked their cars out of sight of the church, there was Reynolds leading his gang of activists down the middle of the road towards the church. To say there was a look of panic on O'Rourke's face is an understatement.

Browne was nominated to act as negotiator for O'Rourke and asked Albert: 'What the fuck are you doing here? This is Westmeath and O'Rourke territory, and you have no fucking business here.'

Reynolds replied that he was entitled to be there as people from nearby Ballymahon (his area) went to Mass in Tang.

Finally, after further heated discussion, an agreement was reached which allowed both candidates to address the Mass-goers.

In retaliation one of O'Rourke's entourage was dispatched to Ballymahon with his vegetable truck adorned with her posters where he drove up and down the street while Reynolds addressed an after-Mass meeting. Reynolds took a dim view of the action.

Fine Gael had three candidates in the field. Outgoing Education Minister Paddy Cooney was joined by Councillor Seamus Finnan and another Mullingar-based barrister, Colm Smith. The PDs were also present with Helena McAuliffe-Ennis.

In the end Fine Gael's vote collapsed and Fianna Fáil won three out of four seats, Albert Reynolds topping the poll with 10,542 first preference votes. Mullingar got a Fianna Fáil TD and Athlone and Longford got a Minister each.

Charles Haughey was appointed Taoiseach, but only on the casting vote of the Ceann Comhairle, Seán Treacy. Albert Reynolds was back in the Department of Industry and Commerce, while Ray MacSharry again took over in Finance.

Reynolds' outgoing, affable personality counterbalanced the more reserved MacSharry, and between them they formed the nucleus of the Cabinet which fought hard to cut back on public expenditure.

Aided by the new Labour Minister, Bertie Ahern, they helped to hammer out an agreement with the social partners in the autumn of 1987 – the Programme for National Recovery (PNR).

The progamme was significant in that it held public pay rises to 2.5 per cent over a three year period and allowed the Government to introduce major cuts in expenditure.

Meanwhile, Albert Reynolds travelled widely in an attempt to woo foreign industrialists. Frequently he was accompanied by the chief executive of the IDA, Padraic White. He later recalled a seminar and lunch for 400 top financiers at the Plaza Hotel in New York in 1987:

'It was a packed, blue-chip audience. We gave a huge presentation. Albert Reynolds laid aside his script and really went for broke. He was right at peak form and he had them eating out of his hand.'

Albert Reynolds had embarked on that four day trip to counteract negative publicity about Ireland in American newspapers. Later the IDA said several American investments in Ireland, including Chase Manhattan in Dublin and Metropolitan Life in Galway, flowed from the trip.

But his chief priority were companies already operating in the Republic.

'There is more emphasis now, since this Government got into office, on putting more effort into natural resources. We should be more selective in what we go for on the national front to fill niches in the economy where we see them,' he said in September '87.

He stressed that when many of the companies were set up by his political hero, Seán Lemass, there was a clear need for them. His approach was to come up with structures that worked rather than operations which just looked good in theory.

'The fact that some bodies did a good job and fulfilled a role for twenty-five years does not mean that they should carry on indefinitely,' he said. 'Maybe some of the bodies could take on new roles.'

While in favour of some privatisation, such as the insurance industry, which he clearly saw as a private sector business, he drew the line at Aer Lingus. 'From the national strategic point of view it would be hard to see the Government of this country leaving it bereft of a national airline,' he said.

As the man concerned with industrial promotion he identified high energy costs, insurance costs, as well as high employer liability costs, as the major bugbears of people in business.

'If Albert Reynolds ever discloses his work schedule to his doctor he'll surely be told that his survival defies the laws of nature,' wrote Brendan Keenan, Business Editor of the *Irish Independent.* 'Since his appointment as Minister for Industry and Commerce he has taken on a staggering workload for the company he believes can be infinitely more profitable – Ireland Ltd. An economic nationalist in the mould of Seán Lemass, Reynolds is the businessman's politician. He detests bureaucracy and firmly believes that this economy simply cannot prosper unless the correct climate for investment exists.'

But the hardworking Minister did end up in hospital for a few days in August 1987 having complained of numbness in his hands and feet. He described the minor complaint as 'difficult to pinpoint'.

In mid '87 Reynolds was confronted with a distasteful industrial strike right in his own town. Worse still, the owner of the factory was his close friend for many years, Longford businessman Noel Hanlon.

– 10 –
Old Friends Are Best

On Tuesday, 14 February 1992, the new Taoiseach Albert Reynolds led his Cabinet team into Dáil Éireann. As he walked behind the Opposition benches towards the Government side of the House, his eye caught sight of a plump, middle-aged man sitting in the front row of the Visitors' Gallery overhead. The Taoiseach immediately smiled and acknowledged the man's presence. The man waved back.

Noel Hanlon was born in Longford in 1940 and left school after his Intermediate Certificate. For two years he worked in the Ford Motor Company in Detroit, but was unimpressed by America which he found totally impersonal, and returned to open his own garage in Longford Town.

When he was approached by Longford County Council with a request to find someone who would do conversion work on ambulances, he found there was nobody in the country equipped to do so. He decided to do it himself. In 1966 he began to assemble ambulances on a small scale, encouraged by the fact that there would always be demand for the product. The success he achieved was phenomenal.

The Six Day War in Israel opened up new markets in the Middle East. A sales drive on Britain's 600 Councils resulted in Hanlon capturing 65 per cent of the British market, but not without being subjected to sneers about the 'Paddy ambulance'.

As he was making a success of his business, his path was mirrored by Albert Reynolds who was running ballrooms and canning petfood. The two became friends when Hanlon sold the future Fianna Fáil leader a second-hand car. Reynolds liked his business acumen. 'Hanlon is as sharp as a computer,' said one Longford man.

It was in Noel Hanlon's villa in Madeira that Albert Reynolds, unable to get Benson & Hedges cigarettes, finally gave up smoking.

But politically the two differed. The Hanlons were well known Fine Gael supporters while the Reynolds brothers, Albert and Jim, were supporters of the Independent TD, Joe Sheridan.

However, as soon as Reynolds opted for politics, Noel Hanlon rowed in behind him, filling the role of finance officer for all his Dáil election campaigns. He was also a key strategist and a key figure behind the winning of three of the four Dáil seats in the 1987 general election.

Hanlon was a no-nonsense operator and was known to give a good dressing down to workers, and indeed to Reynolds himself, for saying and doing things which he believed could lose votes.

As Minister with responsibility for Transport in 1980, Reynolds appointed Noel Hanlon to the Board of Aer Lingus. A qualified pilot, who used to fly to Britain regularly on business trips in his own four-seater plane, Hanlon then sold the plane. He refused the director's fees, but enjoyed the free travel perk which went with the job.

Later he was appointed to the Board of Foir Teoranta, and subsequently became chairman. In 1985 a company which he owned, Manford Clothing and Fashion, had to be bailed out by Foir Teo for £440,000. Hanlon left the boardroom when the decision was taken. When C&D Foods received a large loan from Foir Teo, he once again stepped aside while the decision was taken.

The next Minister, John Bruton, removed Hanlon at the first opportunity in October 1985, having given in to political pressure.

In the mid '80s the ambulance factory – which was now employing 200 – began to suffer. Cutbacks in the health service by the Thatcher Government and the rise in the value of the Punt both hit British sales.

For a trial period the factory operated on a week-on/week-off basis. Subsequently, however, Hanlon decided that the factory would return to full production, but with a loss of eighty-five jobs. Hanlon himself decided who went and who stayed. Seniority and length of service were not criteria, as is normally the case in industrial relations. He insisted the men were only being laid off temporarily.

The issue went to the Labour Court which ruled that the existing work should be shared out among all the workforce either on a week-on/week-off basis or by going on a three day week. Noel Hanlon refused to accept the court's finding and the trade union served notice on Good Friday 1987.

A strike began on 11 May. Hanlon threatened to remove all production to Liverpool where he had a service plant for the British market.

The bitter dispute which followed proved highly embarrassing for Albert Reynolds. While he said he accepted the trade union principle of first in/first out, he maintained that this could not be operated in a factory in which there was a wide range of skills.

The dispute was raised in the Dáil by Workers' Party Deputy, Tomás MacGiolla. Minister for Industry, Albert Reynolds, replied.

When MacGiolla called for the Revenue Commissioners to establish whether the company owed back-taxes, it was too much for the Industry Minister.

He departed from the script prepared by his Department officials and launched into an attack on the Workers' Party. MacGiolla's speech was, he said, inflammatory and despicable. There were plenty of people to represent the people of Longford without MacGiolla trying to stir up trouble.

'If the deputy wants to say Noel Hanlon is a friend of mine, I have 10,542 friends in Longford, and he is one of them,' he declared.

In his account of events, Albert Reynolds claimed that the strike had been taken over by militants, claiming that one member of the strike committee had told some workers that there 'will be no meeting or no talks until Hanlon's is in liquidation'. The strike committee members denied ever making such a statement.

The statement drew the wrath of the ITGWU, whose Vice-President, Eddie Brown, said he was 'appalled' that Mr Reynolds should attempt by 'his comments made under privilege in the Dáil' to justify the actions of an employer whose approach to the dispute had already been judged unreasonable by the Labour Court. He warned that the Minister's comments could have national implications in negotiations with the social partners:

'The Minister's rash attempt to defend the indefensible by making an unjustified attack upon the union is not calculated to enhance the Government's credibility with the trade union movement in its efforts to achieve a consensus on economic recovery.'

In his comments on the union's conduct Albert Reynolds distinguished explicitly between the branch secretary, 'decent' Bob Brady, and the individual trade unionist whom he accused of 'irresponsible' behaviour.

As the owner of C&D Foods Albert Reynolds had had direct dealings with the trade union branch involved in the Hanlon dispute.

A peace plan worked out in talks involving Albert Reynolds and the Bishop of Ardagh and Clonmacnoise, Dr Colm O'Reilly, was rejected by the workers and the plant closed. It was a severe blow to the Minister's home town.

The closure left a bad taste in Longford. In the run-up to the 1989 general election, Reynolds told one aide, pointing to Hanlon, that he would be very much in the background this time. Before the election was over, Hanlon was back in the front line.

'Some of the Mary O'Rourke team tried to make something of the closure. It ran down the runway for them for a bit, but never took off,' said one campaign worker. 'Hanlon was the glue in the campaign team,' added the worker. 'He kept the whole team together. Albert owes him a lot.'

Hanlon kept a low profile for a few years after the factory closure, but in 1990 was appointed by the then EC Agriculture Commissioner,

Ray MacSharry, to the Tobacco Regime Review Committee in Brussels. He has since resigned from the Committee due to pressure of work.

But in the spring of 1994 he was back in the headlines resulting from another appointment by Albert Reynolds, this time as chairman of the VHI.

Hanlon adopted a very much hands-on approach with the VHI and became embroiled in a head-to-head battle with the Board's chief executive, Tom Ryan, over the issue of publishing a list of the names of consultants who did not provide full insurance cover for patients. The Board sided with Hanlon and he remained in control. Ryan accepted an early retirement package.

Hanlon remains a close friend of Albert Reynolds and still turns up in the Visitors' Gallery in the Dáil to watch him in times of political upheaval.

In the summer of 1994 he was appointed chairman of Aer Rianta.

Meanwhile, Albert Reynolds continued to work the countryside attending functions and getting to know people.

For a man who didn't drink, he had a tremendous capacity to stay out late, laughing and gossiping with all and sundry.

During the '70s his cigarette packet was his filofax, every space on the packet filled with scrawled requests to get this or to do that.

In the '80s, when he had stopped smoking, the cigarette packet was replaced by numerous bits of paper which were unloaded from several pockets on to his desk after a visit to the country. This 'bejeepers file' as it was known, was Albert's way of staying close to the grassroots.

Charles Haughey's return to power in 1987 saw the launch of a massive £260,000,000 development of the beef industry to be undertaken by the Goodman Group. It was the biggest programme ever undertaken in the food industry. The plan never took off, but Larry Goodman's name was to feature prominently inside and outside Dáil Éireann for the next seven years.

In April 1988 a series of Dáil questions from Deputy Pat O'Malley of the Progressive Democrats established that Goodman companies had been given massive export credit insurance for their trade with Iraq.

Cover had been withdrawn in 1986 by the Fine Gael Minister for Industry and Commerce, Michael Noonan, because of the high level of risk with the Iraqi economy.

The cover had been granted by Albert Reynolds, but was cancelled again early in 1989 when Ray Burke succeeded him as Minister for Industry and Commerce.

But at the end of 1988 there had been further promotion in store for Albert Reynolds when Finance Minister Ray MacSharry was appointed Ireland's EC Commissioner in succession to Peter Sutherland. MacSharry had signalled that he wanted the top Euro job, but Charles Haughey was reluctant to give it to him because of his value in the Cabinet. When he went to Brussels, Albert Reynolds was promoted to Finance. He was now in the most important Cabinet job, next to the Taoiseach himself.

Reynolds was the obvious choice for the job. During his time in Industry he had helped to revive the economy, principally by driving costs down. In this task he had taken on head-to-head some of the strongest interest groups in the country.

He had been very active in Cabinet, pushing for the abolition of juries in compensation claims in an effort to reduce insurance costs.

He also took on the oil companies by introducing a maximum prices order, and he moved to prevent drink price-fixing, leaving the market to be sorted out through competition.

He had also stepped in to ban 'hello money' and below cost selling in the supermarkets.

'My overall strategy is to take on the powerful lobbies and to do what needs to be done to ensure that the consumer gets a fair deal, whether it be from the oil companies, the publicans or the supermarkets,' he said.

'Mac the Knife may be gone,' but 'Albert Reynolds' axe will be just as sharp,' wrote reporter Gary Culliton in the *Irish Press* shortly after the new Finance Minister's appointment.

In a speech in Longford Albert Reynolds warned that further fiscal rectitude would be the order of the day, despite signs of an economic upturn.

'We are not taking the road toward the cliff top again,' he warned in an attempt to dampen down expectations of tax relief in the January '89 Budget. He warned that the emphasis would be on keeping the level of Government borrowing down.

He also warned that if the country was to 'protect what has been achieved and maintain the new sense of confidence in the economy, further adjustments to the public finances would have to be made.'

The '89 Budget continued on the path of providing the Government's framework for economic and social development.

But Albert Reynolds' first stint in the Department of Finance was cut short by a general election.

On 29 April the Government was defeated in a vote on a Labour party motion calling for £400,000 a year for haemophiliacs who were HIV positive as a result of blood transfusions supplied by the State.

As Cabinet discussion continued on an election, Albert Reynolds was firmly opposed to the idea, along with Gerry Collins and new Cabinet member, Michael Smith. Those in favour were Pádraig Flynn, Ray Burke and Dr Rory O'Hanlon.

'At the final fence I went to sit beside the Taoiseach and pleaded with him not to go to the country,' recalled Reynolds. 'Sleep on it I pleaded.'

But the pleas were in vain. Haughey was finally convinced that the time was ripe to go for an overall majority, something that had eluded him four times previously.

But the Opposition parties were much better prepared for the June 15 election, and Fianna Fáil had underestimated public revulsion at the recently imposed health cuts.

'I remember Albert Reynolds saying at the time that while many people were themselves not directly affected by the health cuts, they probably knew of a neighbour or a respected pensioner in the community who was, and they felt bad about it on that account,' recalled the then Government Press Secretary, PJ Mara. 'Any threat to the health services has a peculiar effect on people in this way. They worry about the future.'

When the votes were counted Fianna Fáil had lost four seats as well as two in the European elections.

Down in Longford-Westmeath Albert Reynolds, while sure of success, had to contend with the thorny issues of a rod-licence dispute and a row over army pay.

Albert had not forgotten his constituency, and in the week before the election brought news of a new factory for Longford Town.

At a high-powered press conference the President of the Brazilian Dona Isabel Corporation, Ricardo Haddad, promised a new factory which would process flax with employment for 340 people by 1990. Mr Haddad said the company had chosen Longford because of the suitability of the region and the 'availability of a high calibre workforce'.

Welcoming the project, Albert Reynolds told the *Longford Leader* that the original contact had come about largely by accident in 1988 when he was Minister for Industry and Commerce.

Asked about the proximity of his Longford visit to the general election, Mr Haddad stated: 'It is a co-incidence'.

The *Longford News*, once owned by Albert Reynolds, saw things rather more simply. 'STROKE' screamed the front page of the pre-election edition of 7 June over a story by reporter Niall Delaney.

Nothing has since been heard of the Dona Isabel Corporation.

Inside the paper of 7 June Delaney reported that Albert Reynolds had managed to visit churches the previous Sunday. One visit to the church in the little village of Tang had to be undertaken with care.

The battle for Tang had been a major source of disagreement between Mary O'Rourke and Albert Reynolds in 1987 as it bordered their territories. But in a typical move Albert mounted the rostrum and told the people on the left-hand side of the village to vote for him, those on the right side for O'Rourke, while those 'over there' (pointing forward) should vote for the third candidate, Henry Abbot.

Later Albert headed for the nuns in Ballymahon Convent. There one sister persisted in questioning him about the upcoming Fianna Fáil Children's Bill and the implications for her pupils. Patience was all that was needed, Albert assured her. It was a complex piece of legislation which needed scrutiny, and was therefore time-consuming.

'But how,' inquired the nun, 'could legislation on the ownership of the Blasket Islands be rushed through the Dáil so quickly?'

'Because there was nothing in it,' came the reply.

Reynolds headed the poll with 9,055 first preference votes, but the party lost their third seat when Henry Abbot was defeated on the sixth and final count. Fine Gael sent two new deputies to Leinster House, Louis Belton and Paul McGrath.

A week later a local youth appeared before Justice Connellan charged with burning a poster of Albert Reynolds and damaging a Telecom Éireann pole to the tune of £50. The youth said he was annoyed as he could not sleep as a result of the noise coming from a disco in a local hotel.

Nationally, Fianna Fáil now had seventy-seven seats and the PDs had six.

In Fianna Fáil Headquarters in Mount Street, PJ Mara was looking at the figures and talking to Charles Haughey.

'Seventy-seven and six make eighty-three. Let's go for it,' he declared.

In the protracted negotiations which followed, Albert Reynolds along with Bertie Ahern negotiated on the Fianna Fáil side, with Bobby Molloy and Pat Cox for the PDs. But the key issues, including the number of Cabinet seats, were worked out between Charles Haughey and Des O'Malley at secret meetings. Later it emerged that Ahern and Reynolds had spent much of the time watching Wimbledon tennis on the TV in their suite as there was nothing else to do.

The drama was added to when Haughey at first refused to resign as Taoiseach. At one stormy meeting Albert Reynolds lost patience with him and demanded that whatever the legal niceties, he should resign. Haughey eventually agreed.

But Haughey had overcome an insurmountable obstacle in entering coalition, something which he privately conceded only he himself could have executed. Even though the PDs got two Cabinet seats, Reynolds had openly said on radio that he believed they were only entitled to one.

But the deal marked the first real signs of a strain in the relationship between Albert Reynolds and Charles Haughey.

Reynolds had been opposed to coalition and had become disillusioned and angry over the way it had been agreed over his head.

'I was naturally hurt that we were not told about the PD Ministers until they had shaken hands with our leader. Haughey and O'Malley devised a formula without our knowledge. It was done behind everybody's back. I was angry at first but then accepted the hard realities of real politics.'

The experience of being treated in this fashion did not come as a total surprise to Reynolds. While he had backed Haughey in three early leadership heaves, a coolness had developed between the two men since 1987, particularly as Reynolds began to emerge as a strong runner in the succession stakes.

In the new Cabinet Haughey's latest confidantes were Ray Burke and Gerry Collins, two men who had voted against him in 1983.

But Albert Reynolds was back in charge of the nation's finances.

Finance Minister, Albert Reynolds, with his budget briefcase outside Leinster House. Left to right: Miriam, Philip, Emer, Kathleen, Albert, Andrea, Leonie, Albert Junior, Cathy. (The Irish Times)

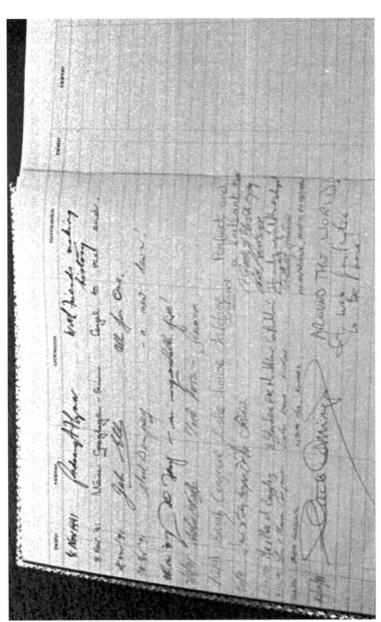

Signatures of Padraig Flynn, Maire Geoghegan Quinn, Noel Dempsey and John Ellis on the register of the Berkeley Court Hotel. (Eamon Farrell/Photocall)

Dublin, January 1993. President Mary Robinson with the Taoiseach Albert Reynolds and Tánaiste Dick Spring in Áras an Uachtaráin after receiving their seals of office. (Derek Speirs/Report).

No 298: Albert Reynolds

Age: 61.

Appearance: Ageing country and western singer with sunbed.

Occupation: Prime Minister and leader of Fianna Fail (Soldiers of Destiny) party.

Isn't he called the Teashop? No Taoiseach, stupid. It's an old Gaelic title for a clan leader, adopted in the 1930s when such terms were briefly fashionable in European politics.

Previous occupation: Dancehall owner. First step up political ladder was a plan to fly wild salmon from Longford to restaurants in Dublin.

Why is he in the news? He's meeting John Major in Dublin today to bring peace to Ireland after 900 years of strife. If all goes well they'll squeeze in a bit of golf after lunch and then go ceilidh dancing with Paisley and the Pope.

John's a big fan of his then? You bet. He's the only world leader who makes Major look interesting.

So his words aren't spoken by a actor on TV? No, but his handlers wish they were.

Surely being Irish he has a way with words? Straight from the Dan Quayle Speech School, I'm afraid. Surprised the Dail last week by saying that he would work for the "cessation of peace in Northern Ireland".

So how did he get where he is? By being a "cute hoor".

What, you mean he put on a short skirt and slept with Charles Haughey? No, that's what the breed of pragmatic parish pump politicians who have run the South for the last 30 years are called.

You mean they promise heaven and earth to get elected and then don't deliver? You're getting the idea.

And the people keep electing them? Not any more, it seems. After a string of corruption scandals, Reynolds' party was forced into coalition earlier this year with Dick Spring's Labour Party, which had campaigned to clean up the corridors of power.

Political style: Back-slapper, the last man to leave the party.

He takes a drink then? No, he's a teetotaller.

Has the man no vices at all? He did once tell a journalist he personally tasted all his company's products before they left the factory. His firm makes dog food.

Secret of his political success: Staying sober in Irish politics.

Political philosophy: What would that be now?

Not to be confused with: Burt Reynolds.

Most likely to say: You finish that bottle of Jamesons first, John, and then we'll talk about peace.

Least likely to say: I think we should re-examine this issue from a post-structuralist perspective.

A profile of Taoiseach, Albert Reynolds, that appeared in 'The Guardian' on 3 December, 1993.

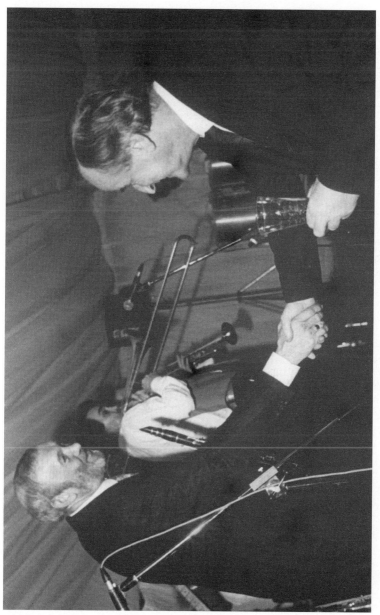

Meeting a familiar face. The Taoiseach Albert Reynolds shakes hands with Paddy Cole at the launching of a new company in Dublin.

John Major and Albert Reynolds shake hands following the signing of their Joint Declaration on the North on 15 December 1993.

(Eamon Farrell/Photocall)

Historic Handshake. Tuesday, 6 September, 1994. Gerry Adams, Albert Reynolds and John Hume shake hands on the steps of Government Buildings. (Eamon Farrell/Photocall)

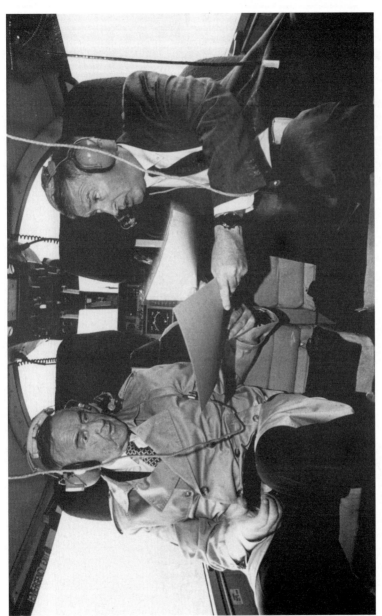

'Do you know how to fly this thing?' Taoiseach Albert Reynolds with Government Press Secretary, Seán Duignan, on a helicopter trip to Mosney in September 1994. (Jon Carlos/Sunday Tribune)

As Ireland prepared to chair the EC during the first half of 1990 Albert Reynolds hoped to be able to convince his counterpart in Britain, John Major, to join the European Monetary System (EMS).

He did not underestimate his task as Minister for Finance.

'People think our problems are over, but we have a £25 billion debt which has to be repaid, that's £2 billion a year just to pay the interest, or £40 a week for everybody who pays tax,' he said in December '89.

Part of the pact with the PDs was to reduce the tax bands, particularly to get the low rate down to 25 per cent by 1993.

He also introduced a system of delegating authority within the civil service.

'"You run your own business," I've told them, and I will get the reductions in public expenditure. In that way you open up areas of responsibility and authority so that they can run their own show and Finance does not have to approve everything.'

He was also very upbeat about the 1990s:

'I see the 1990s as the decade of opportunity, now that we have the economy right. There is an air of confidence and a buzz that we haven't had for years.

'Everybody is looking for opportunities and we are promoting labour-intensive industries like tourism, fishing, mariculture, forestry, indigenous native industries that are a better contributor to the economy than international investment.

'Getting people up and doing . . . that is the kind of modern Ireland I see, what we've done the economists said wouldn't work . . . but we did it anyway.'

Meanwhile, Charles Haughey was in deep trouble in the presidential election which ended with the nightmare scenario of the sacking of the Tánaiste, Brian Lenihan, from office. The loss of the presidential office badly damaged Fianna Fáil, and there were again rumours of a heave against Haughey.

Albert Reynolds cleverly waited in the wings. While avoiding pledging loyalty to Haughey, he made it clear that he would be a candidate for the leadership whenever a vacancy arose.

In the early months of 1991 he came into conflict with the PD chairman Michael McDowell over taxation policy. Reynolds insisted that the cuts being proposed by McDowell could not be introduced without reducing services. He called on 'would-be tax reformers' to spell out what services they would cut if taxes were reduced.

McDowell quickly hit back: 'If Albert Reynolds wants to defend the indefensible I'll take him on anywhere and win,' he declared.

Albert Reynolds had introduced his own unique style to the Department of Finance. The former businessman was ever ready to listen to what business interests had to say and was less likely to take direction from his officials.

He was, on occasions, ready to tackle his own officials, as for example on the issue of property tax. There, he said, a messenger-boy on a bike would be able to identify more quality properties on Adelaide Road than the Revenue Commissioners had selected nationwide.

As he progressed up the political ladder, so too did he modify his behaviour.

By now he had abandoned his more flamboyant ways of living. The days when a distinctive white Mercedes would appear at funerals in his constituency, even if the owner was elsewhere, were no more.

And devils no longer appeared at competing dance-halls in rural areas.

– 11 –
The Ousting

February 16, 1990. Delegates from Fianna Fáil's North Cork Comhairle Ceanntair gathered in Kanturk for a meeting. It was a special meeting where the Minister for Finance, Albert Reynolds, was the guest speaker. The local radio station, County Sound, based in Mallow, noted the visit and sent a reporter to cover the event.

When the Minister spoke, the reporter could scarcely believe his luck. Albert Reynolds delivered a full-powered broadside at coalition with the PDs.

In an unexpected hardline comment he described the coalition as a 'temporary little arrangement' which he hoped would soon be dismantled. His remarks were recorded by the reporter.

'I hope the temporary little arrangement that we have with our junior partners won't be there all that long and we'll be back to where we were,' he declared.

He then went on to claim that the 1990 Budget was put together solely by Fianna Fáil.

'I know that's what Fianna Fáil people wanted me to do and I was proud to do it,' he said.

It was Reynolds' first public comment on coalition, but reflected what he had been thinking for a long time. He had never liked coalition, particularly with the PDs, and he was expressing his hopes for a Fianna Fáil single party government. Reading between the lines there was a clear hint that Albert Reynolds intended to be the man to lead the party to that victory.

Later he defended his comments saying they were made in an organisational context.

'We have our own party. We will be fighting the next election on our own. There's nothing new about that,' he said.

As 1990 drew to a close the tension between Haughey and his Finance Minister increased.

Speaking to reporters in Cork on 10 November, he said he would be a contender for the party leadership in the future:

'If I am around whenever the leadership comes around, my hat will be in the ring.' Such comments clearly irked Haughey.

In Rome for the EC Summit in December, Haughey was asked a question about British financial policy. His reply left Reynolds, who was sitting beside him, ashen-faced:

'We all know that Chancellors of the Exchequer and Ministers for Finance are neurotic and exotic creatures whose political judgment is not always the best.'

Back at home the Government rushed into a new agreement with the social partners, the Programme for Economic and Social Progress (PESP) which provided for public pay costs to rise by nearly 10 per cent a year for three years. Reynolds argued strongly against the deal, but Haughey insisted it went ahead.

After the deal was concluded there were widespread rumours in Leinster House that Labour Minister, Bertie Ahern, wanted to be promoted to Pádraig Flynn's job in Environment. Eventually Haughey issued a statement saying he proposed to leave both men where they were. He followed this up with a minimum reshuffle which brought Brendan Daly back into the Cabinet.

The early months of 1991 were dominated by a new debate on the lowering of the age limit for condoms in new legislation.

At a Cabinet meeting in March Albert Reynolds adamantly opposed lowering the age limit to sixteen. He was supported by Michael O'Kennedy, John Wilson, and Bobby Molloy of the PDs.

However, a subsequent meeting of the Parliamentary Party firmly rejected any change in the law, and Haughey abandoned his plans.

'I for one am prepared to give the benefit of the doubt to the present leader in that he genuinely believed in his initial proposals for a liberalisation of the current nonsensical laws,' wrote backbench Deputy Charlie McCreevy in *The Irish Times*. 'But yet again the illiberal, Roman Catholic dominant element of the party soon whipped the Dáil deputies into line . . . The current party hierarchy believes that to obtain consistently a first preference national vote in the mid to high forties means that you do not alienate the gombeen culture, and cute hoorism is their motto.'

Meanwhile, Albert Reynolds and his supporters were quietly preparing their ground for a take-over of the leadership.

While they had originally planned to wait for Charles Haughey to stand aside, as the months of 1991 dragged on it became clear that they would have to pressurise the Taoiseach into stepping down.

The central players in the Reynolds camp were Pádraig Flynn, Maire Geoghegan-Quinn, Noel Treacy and Michael Smith. There were frequent reports of Flynn visiting Albert Reynolds' Ballsbridge apartment. This group was quickly named the 'country 'n' western' alliance by its opponents.

Reynolds had also been promised the support of Bertie Ahern, the key man in Dublin, but only when Haughey decided to step aside himself. There was an informal understanding between the two that Reynolds would serve for five or six years to be followed by Ahern. This so-called 'dream ticket' of Reynolds and Ahern was seen to unite the urban and rural strands of Fianna Fáil.

In the Autumn of 1991 Reynolds made it increasingly clear again that he would be a contender for the leadership.

For example, speaking in Fermoy on 17 September he said: 'You can take it that whenever a vacancy occurs, my name will be there. At present, there is none, but if one arises, I will be interested.'

When Ministers returned after the summer recess Albert Reynolds openly showed his opposition to Haughey.

He insisted to the Cabinet that the terms of the PESP would have to be renegotiated and told RTE's Sunday programme, *This Week*, that it could not be paid in full.

Press Secretary PJ Mara immediately rejected Reynolds' comments as 'the usual Department of Finance rhetoric'.

Mara later chalked down 1 September 1991 as the beginning of the end for Haughey. It marked the opening of the last and most difficult chapter in Mara's job as Government Press Secretary.

Over the next six months life would become for him one long litany of explanations and counter-explanations, leading from crisis to crisis.

By now the Government was swallowed up in a new controversy over the Sugar Company. *Sunday Independent* journalist Sam Smyth had revealed that its chief executive, Chris Comerford, was suing the directors of a Jersey-based company, Talmino, which had sold its stake in a subsidiary of the Sugar Company, Irish Sugar Distributors. Comerford was claiming he had a stake in Talmino.

The Greencore controversy was complicated by the Beef Tribunal saga and a new Telecom controversy over a proposed headquarters site in Ballsbridge when it was discovered that the chairman, Dr Michael Smurfit, had a share in the company which sold the site to Telecom.

'There was a period in September 1991 when some people were getting restless,' says PJ Mara. 'It was nothing you could put your finger on, but it was around.'

Mara says Reynolds' comments really annoyed Haughey and many other members of the Government.

Haughey alarmed Ministers and backbenchers alike when he jokingly commented on RTE radio that 'some of these Chinese leaders go on until they are 80 or 90, but I think that's probably a bit long'.

The pressure increased on Haughey when four backbench deputies – MJ Nolan, Noel Dempsey, Liam Fitzgerald and Seán Power

– issued a statement expressing their disquiet over the handling of recent events.

At a subsequent Parliamentary Party meeting, two of them, Power and Dempsey, told Haughey he should go. Haughey fought on, narrowly surviving a 'no confidence' motion in the Dáil.

In his article in *The Irish Times* on 31 October, old Haughey foe Charlie McCreevy expressed concern about the future of Fianna Fáil.

'No more than a decade ago, the accolade of the greatest political organisation in the democratic free world was commonly ascribed to the (Fianna Fáil) party by friend and foe alike,' he wrote. 'Now not even the diehard of the diehard Fianna Fáiler believes such a description to be accurate . . . The proud boast that Fianna Fáil was not a political party but a national movement is no longer sustainable. Changing leaders will not solve the problems of Fianna Fáil. The party needs direction – any direction.'

Spelling out the party's problems, McCreevy argued that the party no longer reflected the make-up of Irish society, nor was it in any way in tune with the changes in that society.

'The pressure of the recent party hiatus caused one faction to ascribe the appellation "country and western" to their opponents. It was not meant either as a compliment or a well thought-out contribution, but it inadvertently summarised the image problem of the Fianna Fáil party as seen through the eyes of most non-believers. The image will stick to the party for so long as it has this inherent imbalance in the social make-up of the organisation.'

McCreevy concluded his article by saying: 'I would hate to be remembered as being in that generation of Fianna Fáil deputies who were there at the deathbed of a once so great and proud party.'

The widely-read article reflected the dilemma facing the party and the worries of many of its backbench deputies.

Finally, on 6 November, McCreevy's constituency colleague, Seán Power, the son of former Haugheyite, Defence Minister Paddy Power, tabled a motion for the Parliamentary Party requesting the deputies to 'discontinue forthwith the leadership of Charles J Haughey'.

Albert Reynolds, who heard about the motion as he was being driven to a function in Newtowncashel, Co Longford, was faced with a tough choice.

'I was in Newtowncashel for a Tidy Towns meeting when I heard the news,' he said. 'Eddie Bohan phoned me in the car. I knew the pressure was on me then. I came back to Dublin, told Bertie Ahern and P Flynn that I would be supporting the motion. I did not want to be labelled a hypocrite. I knew I was going to be sacked.'

He also told John Wilson, Ray Burke, Seamus Brennan and Brendan Daly. 'I couldn't contact Mary O'Rourke or Gerry Collins. Bertie Ahern tried to talk me out of it.'

The timing did not suit Reynolds as he knew the motion was unlikely to succeed. He issued the following statement:

'For some time now there has been considerable political instability which has led to an erosion of confidence in our democratic institutions. This uncertainty must not be allowed to continue. The well-being of our country requires strong and decisive leadership of Government and of the Fianna Fáil party. I am not satisfied that such leadership now exists. In the circumstances I will be supporting the motion tabled for the party meeting on next Saturday.'

A brief car telephone conversation with the Taoiseach shortly after 7.00 pm on the evening of 5 November ended his post as Minister for Finance.

Earlier, on the *RTE Six o'clock News* he had missed one of the most bizarre performances ever by a Fianna Fáil Minister when Gerry Collins had predicted Albert Reynolds would 'wreck our party right down the middle and bust up the Government'.

While some of his family had recorded the Collins' interview, Albert Reynolds has refused to look at it ever since. But it was a performance he would never forget.

Environment Minister P Flynn was also sacked when he came out in support of the motion. Junior Ministers Maire Geoghegan-Quinn, Michael Smith and Noel Treacy also supported the motion.

'With friends making history,' wrote P Flynn, somewhat prematurely, in the register of the Berkeley Court Hotel where the sacked Ministers met on 8 November, 1991.

The Fianna Fáil meeting on Saturday, 9 November, lasted fourteen and a half hours during which time Charles Haughey never once left the room.

In his contribution Reynolds claimed he had been the victim of a campaign of misinformation, and he laid the blame at the door of the Government Press Secretary.

He also surprised those present with his claim that a white Hiace van had been spotted acting suspiciously near his Ballsbridge apartment.

Party chairman Jim Tunney intervened and a special commission was set up to inquire into the allegations. It consisted of Jim Tunney, John Wilson and Albert Reynolds.

The general view from the meeting was that Albert Reynolds had gone over the top in his complaints, and it became glaringly obvious that Haughey would have a major victory.

PJ Mara dismissed Albert Reynolds' entire claims.

'My only comment is that nobody ever spoke to me except Jim Tunney. The whole thing about Hiace vans and a campaign of misinformation was absolute and total rubbish.'

When the vote was called Haughey had again survived by fifty-five votes to twenty-two.

As the Ministers departed Leinster House the mob outside the gates chanted: 'Albert's in a Lada'.

But they quickly had to swallow their taunts as, within hours, Albert Reynolds was driving a sleek new navy-coloured Jaguar, a £50,000 present from his family it was claimed.

The failure of the car to be registered until January was the subject of a Dáil question to the new Environment Minister Michael Smith in May '92. The Minister assured the House that the car had only been taken for one test drive in November and had been garaged until early January.

Down in Longford nothing much had changed, with his supporters now believing Albert Reynolds had firmly staked his claim on the Fianna Fáil leadership.

An elderly man at the bar in Kelly's public house on Longford's Main Street told *The Irish Times* that although he had been a Fianna Fáil supporter all his life, he now wanted to see an end to the Haughey era.

'Do you know any Government in any democratic country in the world that could tell its people who the head of the next Government is going to be? Well, according to Charles Haughey, he is going to tell us. He seems to forget that there has been free education in Ireland now for over twenty years.'

Frank Whitney, the Secretary of Mostrim Fianna Fáil Cumann, worked at C&D Foods for over twenty years.

'Albert Reynolds is tough, fair and decisive,' he said. 'I get nothing for nothing from him. I work hard and he expects me to work hard. That is the kind of leader this country needs.'

Seán Glennon, the chairman of the Ballinalee Comhairle Ceanntair, said people were coming up to him asking him to thank Albert Reynolds for allowing them to hold their heads up again.

'If Albert Reynolds becomes leader, the true Fianna Fáil people will be back,' he said.

Meanwhile, Albert and Kathleen Reynolds headed off to the sun for a ten-day break in Maspalomas on Grand Canaria.

Back in Leinster House Charles Haughey caused a major surprise when he appointed two backbench TDs, Noel Davern and Dr Jim McDaid, as replacements in Cabinet for the sacked Albert Reynolds and Pádraig Flynn. McDaid withdrew before his official appointment following the release by the Workers' Party of a photograph of him beside a leading IRA man, James Pius Clarke, during the hearing of Clarke's extradition case. McDaid had made it clear that he supported the Government policy on extradition, but the appointment was seen as insensitive. The saga further weakened Haughey's position.

Albert Reynolds had by now embarked on a tour of the country. He began with a speech in the little village of Williamstown in Co Galway. Re-echoing Charlie McCreevy's words, he said the party faithful no longer understood what the party stood for.

'Fianna Fáil stands for the co-operative and humane working of the economy and of society for the good of all and not for a chosen few,' he declared.

Fianna Fáil alone could provide the direction, leadership and unifying force in Irish society which was 'essential to the future of our country'. But he warned that this could only be achieved if the aims and ideals are properly understood and are seen to be relevant to all, particularly the young.

As Albert Reynolds was touring the country, a key event was about to take place in a pub in Castlerea, Co Roscommon.

Having failed to win a Dáil seat in the general election of 1989, Seán Doherty was working his way quietly back up the political ladder. Elected to the Seanad he was now Cathaoirleach, but his ambition was to return to the Cabinet table.

He was still angry that he had had to take responsibility for the tapping of the telephones of two journalists, Geraldine Kennedy and Bruce Arnold back in 1982. When the Minister for Justice, Ray Burke, published in 1992 a Bill dealing with legislation to govern phone-tapping, Doherty decided he had taken enough.

He chose a pub in his own Roscommon constituency, Hell's Kitchen in Castlerea, owned by Seán and Ann Browne, for the launch.

'Friday, January 10, will go down in the history books as the day when the former Cathaoirleach of the Seanad, Seán Doherty, dropped the first hint that GUBU was returning with a vengeance, the day when the preparations began for the serving up of Charlie Haughey's head on a plate,' wrote Christina McHugh in the *Roscommon Herald*.

'The crowd in Hell's Kitchen on that historic Friday night were unaware that they were watching history in the making as the cameras rolled, and RTE's *Nighthawks* team recorded the Doc's comments for transmission on the following Wednesday, January 15.'

The Cathaoirleach was asked if he had taken the rap for Haughey in the phone-tapping affair in 1982. He replied:

'No, the situation was at that time I had a job to do – there was a decision in Cabinet that the prevention of the leaking of matters from Cabinet must be stopped. I, as Minister for Justice, had a direct responsibility for doing that – I did that. I don't feel that I was let down by the fact that people knew what I was doing.'

Eighteen days before, on 23 December, Doherty had made the same comment in an interview on Shannonside Radio, but nobody noticed. After the *Nighthawks* programme, presenter Shay Healy asked Doherty over a pint if there was anything he had said that he didn't want transmitted.

'No,' replied Doherty, 'but I said something significant there.'

Today the yellow painted chair on which Seán Doherty sat when he made those comments has become the centre of attention. Visitors still want to see where it all began.

The *Nighthawks* comments were leaked to the *Irish Press* before being transmitted and the programme hit the headlines.

Doherty maintained his silence for a few days. There was much speculation that he was a stalking horse for Albert Reynolds who knew that time was not on his side.

But Reynolds insisted he had been unaware of the *Nighthawks* programme, and only got to know of its contents when he received a phone call from his media adviser, Tom Savage.

'The balloon is about to go up with Doherty,' said Savage.

'Holy Jesus, I don't think we need this,' replied Reynolds.

'I had nothing good, bad or indifferent to do with that. Nor had anyone acting on my behalf anything to do with Doherty either,' Reynolds said later. 'It certainly did not serve any useful purpose since I think it did further harm to the party. It certainly harmed my campaign and only the electorate will decide in time if it did Seán Doherty's political career any harm or not.'

Not everybody believed him.

But the Albert Reynolds camp were monitoring events closely.

'There was a core of twenty-two who had been in the trenches and were watching developments,' Environment Minister Michael Smith told the *Sunday Tribune*.

On 21 January following a visit to Spain, Doherty called a hastily prepared press conference and brushed aside any vagueness about his comments on the *Nighthawks* programme.

'I am confirming tonight that the Taoiseach, Mr Haughey, was fully aware in 1982 that two journalists' phones were being tapped, and that he at no stage expressed a reservation about this action,' Doherty read from a prepared script.

According to his version of events, he had taken the transcripts of the tapes and given them to Haughey personally and left them in his possession.

'At no stage did he indicate disapproval of the action which had been taken,' he added.

Doherty announced he would be resigning his position as Cathaoirleach and left the press conference without answering a single question.

The PDs held an emergency meeting and decided they could no longer support a Haughey Government.

Haughey fought back, answering questions at a press conference for over an hour. But it was too late.

Even before Haughey decided to relinquish office on the night of Wednesday, 22 January, the Reynolds camp were already sure of at least thirty-nine votes.

As soon as Doherty made his statement the camp swung into overdrive. Each member was given a number of deputies to 'mind'.

Michael Smith was 'in charge of' Brendan Kenneally of Waterford; Michael Ahern of Cork East; Dan Wallace and Denis Lyons of Cork North Central; Micheal Martin and John Dennehy of Cork South Central; Tom McEllistrim of Kerry North and John O'Leary of Kerry South.

Noel Dempsey was 'in charge of' Joe Jacob, Wicklow; Willie O'Dea, Limerick East; Seamus Kirk, Louth; Tom Kitt, Dublin South; John O'Connell, Dublin South Central; Liam Hyland, Laois Offaly and Dermot Fitzpatrick, Dublin Central.

Charlie McCreevy soon joined in and the 'minders' were swapped around to counter-check. Meetings took place in Dáil offices, in Jury's Hotel and in Michael Smith's Dublin home at 2 Victoria Terrace, Donnybrook.

Two other candidates, Mary O'Rourke and Dr Michael Woods, declared, while Finance Minister Bertie Ahern did his sums.

'I have to say that I'm not ambitious and I never was,' Reynolds said at the time. 'I am making this bid to be leader because, quite frankly, I believe I am the best at this time. I'm not a man for intrigue, and as a leader I would be what I have always been as a backbencher and a Minister – straight-up, accessible, in that what you see is what you get.'

During the race with Ahern, Albert Reynolds showed himself capable of brutal wit. He sympathised with the Finance Minister's domestic difficulties, but then added, apparently casually, 'people do like to know where the Taoiseach of the day is living'. It reminded some of the comment he is said to have made about Charles Haughey: 'He seems to think he will be able to leave Fianna Fáil to his sons in his will'.

On 1 February Ahern telephoned Reynolds and arranged a meeting. The venue was the Skylon Hotel in Drumcondra. Reynolds travelled alone. There they discussed their individual support and the weather! They arranged to meet again in the afternoon, this time in the Oak pub in Finglas.

Having spoken for a few minutes Bertie called in his close friend, Councillor Tony Kett, and told him he was supporting Reynolds for Taoiseach.

'At that time I knew I was there,' said Reynolds. 'I reckoned I would have fifty-five or fifty-six.'

Shortly before 3.00 pm on Thursday 6 February Albert Reynolds drove his new Jaguar through the back entrance to Leinster House and parked in the members' carpark on the left-hand side.

But already the visitors' bar was full of Longford people, including most of the Reynolds family.

Local Councillor, Peter Kelly, agreed that there would be a happy hour in his pub on Longford's Main Street.

'It's the day to have it,' he declared. 'Everybody's in Dublin.'

The atmosphere was slightly tense as news spread that Dr Michael Woods had sent out a personal letter and was mounting a strong campaign at the eleventh hour.

Suddenly Albert Reynolds appeared.

A huge cheer went up. Looking well but slightly nervous, Albert waved to the fans. Then he was gone.

Leitrim TD Gerry Reynolds was on his feet in the Dáil Chamber speaking on *'Financial Motions (Resumed, Motion 22)'* as the Fianna Fáil Parliamentary Party meeting began.

Within half an hour a whisper began to sweep through the corridors, 'No contest, no contest'.

Party chairman Jim Tunney appeared on the plinth in front of Leinster House and announced the news: '61, 10, 6. Reynolds.'

A deafening roar followed. House Superintendent Eamon O'Donoghue appealed for restraint.

'Please now, respect the dignity of the House,' he pleaded.

Jim Tunney lent a hand.

'The House is in session, please respect the dignity of the House. This is not a county championship,' he said loftily.

'Drinks on the House,' shouted a Longford voice. An emotional Mickey Doherty hugged an equally emotional Reynolds supporter Benny Reid.

But the new Fianna Fáil leader had fled via a side entrance to his home in Ballsbridge to tell his wife Kathleen the good news. Then it was on to Jury's Hotel for a press conference.

There he read a short statement thanking his supporters and briefly outlined his views on the future. Then it was off to the Dáil again, the Fianna Fáil National Executive and a party for the Longford contingent in the Tara Towers Hotel.

On Friday, 7 February, Albert and Kathleen Reynolds moved into the Berkeley Court Hotel in Ballsbridge. He needed some time to finalise his Cabinet and Ministers of State.

'With pen and paper I wrote down dozens of names,' he said. 'I crossed some of the names out, put new ones in, brought old ones back. Then I would leave it there, watch television, have a meal, talk to some people and at times consult Kathleen.'

On Saturday night he finalised his team.

'I was aware I had to establish that I was my own man. There is no room for sentiment in politics.'

On Sunday evening Reynolds rang the PD leader Des O'Malley and invited him to his suite. There he showed him his new line-up.

'Hmm...there's certainly some interesting changes there,' remarked O'Malley. The PD leader was not impressed at the dropping of so many experienced Ministers.

'I knew that Bertie was the anchor man and Máire had to be in there,' Albert told Michael Hand of the *Sunday Tribune*. 'She should never have been outside Cabinet. Flynn and Smith were talented and brave in November. David Andrews was a very early choice for me, top of the new people.'

When David Andrews answered his phone in his Blackrock home, Reynolds told him he was giving him 'F.A.'. Andrews laughed at the ambiguous wording.

'John O'Connell is a kind and caring man and anybody who wanted that job (Health) as badly as he did I felt should be given a run. The other new people, Joe Walsh, Brian Cowen, Charlie McCreevy, had always impressed me.'

Seamus Brennan told Reynolds that he felt Education was wrong for him.

'I told him that Eamon de Valera and Jack Lynch had held that position, and he accepted in a flash.'

On Tuesday, 11 February, Charles Haughey announced his resignation to a hushed Dáil. The formal tributes paid, Albert Reynolds was nominated for Taoiseach and quickly voted in with the support of the Progressive Democrats.

Twenty minutes after his return from Áras an Uachtaráin where he received his seal of office from President Robinson, he had a thankless task to perform.

Sitting in John Wilson's office he summoned in eight of his former Cabinet colleagues to tell them they would not be serving with him.

Noel Davern, the Minister for Education, was first in.

The new Taoiseach looked up from behind his desk and said: 'I won't be asking you to serve in Government . . .' That was it. Noel Davern, cool and courteous, thanked him and left. He was outside the door in seconds.

The new Taoiseach told Gerry Collins he found it hard to imagine a Fianna Fáil Cabinet without him, but he would not be in his Government.

When Albert Reynolds told Justice Minister Ray Burke he would not be on his Cabinet team he added that his door would always be open.

'That's all right. I won't be needing it,' replied Burke.

The other Ministers came and went, saying little. Mary O'Rourke told him what she thought of her sacking, and Dermot Ahern confronted him about the unfairness of his sacking as Chief Whip.

Those who were being sacked were obliged to wait in the same room as those receiving office.

'It was a hanging – it was quite awful,' said one of those dismissed.

Former Government Press Secretary PJ Mara had often joked that you should follow the maxim: 'In defeat, magnanimity; in victory vengeance.' That was how it appeared to the new losers.

This task complete, the Taoiseach summoned in the new Ministers who had not yet been told of their appointments.

It was all just beginning.

– 12 –
Kathleen

Thursday, 6 February 1992. Seven o'clock in the morning. The first television crew arrived at the Reynolds' luxury apartment in Dublin's Ballsbridge. It was the day of the critical Fianna Fáil Parliamentary Party meeting to elect a new leader.

Kathleen Reynolds was already up and about, busily making tea and answering the telephone.

There was a flurry of excitement shortly after 8.00 am when youngest son, Albert Junior, arrived unexpectedly from New York where he works for Chase Manhattan Bank on Wall Street.

The previous evening he had managed to fool his mother on the telephone.

'Be sure to call me the minute you hear any news,' he warned her.

Daughter Cathy arrived in the kitchen.

'I think we're in for a long day, Mum,' she remarked.

'A long day?' repeated her mother. 'It's going to be the longest day of my life.'

As the time for the meeting approached, all the girls in turn kissed Albert.

As he kissed Kathleen he said: 'You'll be proud of me before this day is out'.

'You know I'm very proud of you, love. We all are. Good luck and God bless, Albert,' she replied.

An agonising forty-six minutes later at 3.31 pm the newsflash came through of Albert's landslide victory. A huge cheer went up in the Reynolds' living room.

'Thank God,' prayed a relieved Kathleen Reynolds out loud. 'It's finally over.'

'If anything ever calls for a celebration, this does,' she said.

Recovering from a cancer illness she said that, although she had been a teetotaller all her life, her doctors had told her to have the odd glass of sherry or champagne for medicinal purposes.

And her verdict on her first glass of bubbly?

'I like it. It's very refreshing.'

The arrival within minutes of the Garda Chief Superintendent from nearby Donnybrook Station with two security guards was the first sign of the new lifestyle as a Taoiseach's wife.

Albert himself arrived complete with his former ministerial driver, Phil Riley, and a back-up security car.

The following Tuesday Kathleen Reynolds was with her sister in the Distinguished Visitors' Gallery when her beloved Albert was voted Taoiseach of the land.

Always a lover of fashion, she was dressed in a smart black, white and red bouclé tweed outfit by Escada, which she had bought on impulse the previous Christmas in Richard Alan's.

'I never got to wear it at all then,' she told *Irish Independent* journalist Angela Phelan. 'When I bought it I noticed that there was a pair of lovely matching red and black suede gloves. But they were very expensive and I felt that I had already spent enough. I mentioned them to the girls when I came home, but I never gave them another thought until Christmas morning when I opened my presents. Albert had bought them for me.'

'Political wives like Kathleen Reynolds don't exist in American politics,' wrote Brenda Power in the *Sunday Press*. 'That is why you've got the spectacle of Barbara Bush and Hilary Clinton racing each other to the kitchen stove to turn out another batch of chocolate chip cookies and banging on about the kids and the dogs and the detergent that gets his shirts bluey-white. But the difference between

Kathleen and the Barbaras and the Hilarys is that Kathleen is for real. She's the genuine article.'

A typical mother she worries about her children, their exams, politics, everything.

'I'm the worrier,' Kathleen told Brenda Power, 'always down on my knees asking God for favours . . . it's part of my make-up. I'm forever worrying about them all. People have this image of me as being bubbly, but somebody has to do the worrying.'

Her influence in the home is immense.

'I am the boss in the house,' she told the *Longford Leader* in an interview in 1987. 'I am here all of the time and discuss things with the children. Their ambition is something which they inherited from their father and not me.'

Kathleen's influence on Albert Reynolds is immense, and extends to consultation with her on most matters. However, apparently they did not discuss the £1,000,000 Masri investment in C&D. Her view on the make-up of his first Cabinet, for example, was given serious consideration. Long the key figure behind Albert Reynolds, rarely – other than possibly Joan FitzGerald – has a wife had so much influence on a Taoiseach.

'He likes to have my support, and he thinks it important, but I wondered at the start how I was going to attend all those functions,' she said.

Kathleen Reynolds looks at the economy as a housewife would look at her budget – and she has observed, 'My bank manager would not be very happy if I was in the same situation as the Government'.

The political rat race is carried onto foreign trips, she says.

'It sounds beautiful staying in an exotic hotel while on business, but Albert comes home saying he never saw the outside of the hotel. I know myself that everything is organised. You are like a zombie rushing against the clock, and you leave the country without having seen anything. It is all high-powered stuff, and private holidays are few and far between.'

Kathleen Coen had first met Albert Reynolds when she worked in McGettrick's Outfitters on O'Connell Street Ballymoate. He was the local CIE goods clerk.

'He was a new man in town and all the girls in the shop were interested in him,' she said later. 'In those days very few strangers came to town, and he was a great cause of excitement.'

Kathleen's father, Philip Coen, died from multiple sclerosis in 1958. She missed him terribly.

'He was a big influence on me. The values and the sense of family that I have now come from him and from my mother, Bridget, God rest them.'

In 1910 the young Phil Coen had run away from a small Sligo farm. He settled in Philadelphia and joined the US army at the outbreak of World War 1. He saw action on the Austrian/German border and after demobilisation in 1918 returned to his native Cuffada.

'He was a very proud man,' said Kathleen. 'He would lead in reciting the rosary in the kitchen every night.'

Her abiding memory of him was during the time before electricity when he would read to them using an oil lamp.

They were not a wealthy family.

'We hadn't a car, just a lovely pony and trap. But my Dad was the sort of person who loved to have the best bullock at the fair.'

Albert and Kathleen were married on 19 June, 1962, in Dublin's Westland Row Church, a year after he had packed up his CIE job and opted for the ballroom business full-time.

The wedding was a simple affair with just sixty guests. Albert's older brother, Jim, was the best man and one of Kathleen's cousins, Norrie Kenny, was bridesmaid.

After the wedding ceremony the couple and their guests drove out to the Grand Hotel in Malahide for the reception. The honeymoon was a two week holiday in Majorca.

For the first few months of their married life Albert and Kathleen lived with his mother in Rooskey, before they bought their own home 'Mount Carmel' on the Dublin Road in Longford. The house was bought mainly on the proceeds of a ballroom tour by Kenny Ball and his Jazzmen who had a number one hit with *Midnight in Moscow.* Albert Reynolds paid £4,500 in cash.

During the early years of their married life Kathleen travelled a lot with Albert to the ballrooms to help with the running of the dances.

In 1964 their first child, Miriam, was born and Kathleen became a full-time homemaker.

The other children – Philip, Emer, Leonie, Albert Junior, Cathy and Andrea – followed quickly. Kathleen hired a full-time house-helper who moved in with the family. At one stage all seven children were under ten years of age.

'My earliest memories are of Sunday drives with him,' said Leonie Reynolds, who is right in the middle of the family. 'He was working a lot and travelling during the week, so we would all cherish the spin on Sunday.

'He would sing songs and we weren't long learning them. I can just about remember them. There was one about a red hen and one of his favourites was "Two little boys had two little toys".'

The children went to national school locally but later they all went to boarding school. Miriam was given the choice of going to day school or boarding school. When she chose to board, the others followed her.

'There was no pressure on any of us,' said Emer. 'Philip couldn't wait to get into the business.'

Mrs Reynolds was always there to help the children with their homework when they were at national school.

'Mum would give us a spelling test and she would correct our homework,' Emer told *Irish Times* journalist Renagh Holohan. 'She was always there, she was our teacher at home. She took great interest.'

The five girls attended La Sainte Union Convent, a French Order of nuns in Banagher, Co Offaly, while Philip and Albert Junior went to the Cistercian College in Roscrea.

Their mother was a frequent visitor to the schools, driving the hundred miles to see how they were doing and to talk to their teachers.

As the family grew older Albert rented a house in Galway every year for a month's holiday. He worked during the week and went to stay with them at weekends.

But the final week's holidays he took himself and he always arranged for it to coincide with the Galway Races, his main sporting indulgence.

The family have always been extremely close and frequently the extended family of twelve or thirteen will go out for dinner together.

Albert Reynolds listens to what his children say to him.

'Dad does not bring his work home with him,' said Emer. 'When we are all sitting down we would say this is good or this is bad. We are giving him a little bit of feedback. He loves to hear what others are thinking. Cathy and Andrea would tell him what the young people think in UCD and he likes to listen to that.'

Leonie recalled that friends were always welcome.

'When we would bring home our friends, it didn't matter who would be with our parents, everyone would always be made welcome and included in the conversation.'

Over the years Kathleen became a lover of the sun, particularly the Far East. Hong Kong, Singapore and Bangkok became some of her favourite places, and both she and Albert have been back many times.

Hotel managers in Spain could not believe that the nine were all members of one big family.

Meanwhile, Albert and Kathleen gradually extended the family home in Longford. A swimming pool was added.

In October 1979 Kathleen hosted a lunch for the then Health Minister Charles Haughey in her home when he paid a visit to Manor

Nursing Home. Guests at the table included Noel Hanlon. Mrs Reynolds was assisted by local friend Mrs Pádraig Connellan, and Albert's private secretary, Averil Fitzgerald.

If Hilary Clinton is famous for her chocolate-chip cookies, then Kathleen Reynolds can as easily claim fame for her tasty cheesecake.

The Health Minister tucked into smoked salmon, lobster soup, Longford roast, with lemon cheesecake for desert. So taken was Haughey with Kathleen's cheesecake that he asked her to send him the recipe.

The recipe was as follows:

4 oz of digestive biscuits
2 oz of butter
1 level tablespoonful castor sugar.
Filling – one quarter pint of double cream; 6 oz of condensed milk;
2 large lemons.
Topping – lightly whipped double cream; fresh lemon slices.
Oven setting: gas mark 2.

Method: Crush biscuits. Melt butter in pan. Add sugar and blend with biscuits. Mix well. Turn mix into a 7-inch pie plate and press into shape round base and sides of plate with back of spoon. Bake for eight minutes in slow oven. Remove from the oven and cool. Mix cream, condensed milk and grated lemon rind. Pour into a flan case and chill for several hours.

'This "do" in Albert Reynolds' house will become more famous than the Boston Tea Party,' said one letter in the *Longford News* the following week.

And the writer, who signed himself 'Fish and Chips' added the following observation:

'The recipe is correct, but in some houses on the Dublin Road they grate a half-pound of Cheddar cheese into a saucepan, add an ounce of butter and a naggin of white wine before bringing it to the boil and letting it simmer for ten minutes. It is supposed to give cheesecake the proper tang.'

In the early '80s Albert bought an apartment, No 2 Laurel, Hazeldene, just off Anglesea Road in Ballsbridge. It was a luxury apartment which overlooked the Merrion Cricket Club.

Some years later in 1987 while Minister for Industry and Commerce he moved to a bigger apartment in the same complex which he purchased for £150,000. It was twice the size of the first one which he sold for £80,000.

During the period in the run-up to his election as leader of Fianna Fáil the Reynolds girls acted as *ad hoc* press officers for their father.

'We were answering the phone and sending faxes. We were acting as spokespersons for him,' said Emer. 'We all got totally involved. I think I know every journalist. Even *Sky News* were asking for us by name. They found it unusual not to have civil servants dealing with him.'

The family have been an enormous asset to Albert Reynolds, and his daughters frequently deputise with absolute ease for their mother at official functions or trips abroad.

'Albert and Kathleen were very lucky to have such a nice family,' says long-time family friend Paddy Cole. 'They are all a lovely bunch with great personalities.'

Since 1992 when he was appointed Taoiseach the Gardaí have a permanent security hut outside the apartment.

But there were some red faces in February 1994 when thieves broke into the apartment next to that of the Taoiseach. That apartment is owned by Jenny Hanley, widow of Albert Reynolds' life-long friend Peter Hanley of Rooskey. Mrs Hanley was knocked to the ground when she surprised the thieves shortly before 8.00 pm in the evening. The incident led to a review of security at the complex.

In December 1991 Kathleen Reynolds discovered she had cancer.

It was the evening of the Cairde Fáil dinner following Albert's dismissal from office. She will never forget it.

'I'd an ache in my shoulder, my upper arm,' she said. 'Albert came in and he said: "Oh, Lord, are you not ready yet?" I said, "Sure I've still got to have my shower", and that's when I found the lump, the size of a golf ball in my armpit . . . so I showed it to Cathy, and we rang the doctor that night.'

But she went with Albert to the Cairde Fáil dinner. This writer saw them arrive at the Burlington Hotel, late. Taoiseach Charles Haughey was already speaking and they had to wait outside the door of the function room until he was finished.

The next morning Kathleen's doctor returned and told her he was sending her into hospital on the following Tuesday.

As soon as the biopsy was taken she expected to go home. But the specialist in the Mater Private Hospital broke the bad news to her. The biopsy was malignant and urgent surgery was necessary. Kathleen Reynolds was shocked.

'I just couldn't believe that this was happening to me. The staff were wonderful, but I cried for the rest of the evening. I didn't know just what lay ahead for me. I've always enjoyed clothes and I just couldn't imagine how I was going to look with a breast removed. I suppose it was as much fear of the unknown that upset me at that time because I just didn't know what I was facing . . . I've always been a great believer in the power of prayer and I prayed for most of the night. I silently prayed to St Rita of Cascia. Over the years I had asked her for little favours, like exam success for the children and the like, and she never let us down.'

On Thursday she underwent the operation.

'I was delighted at how well I felt immediately after surgery. I had expected to be in pain, but I really had very little discomfort. The doctor had explained that, depending on the outcome of the surgery,

I would most likely have to have some chemotherapy treatment, a prospect I found daunting.'

Just a few days later it started.

For six weeks she went into hospital every Sunday evening, returning home on Tuesday. With the chemotherapy went the usual side-effects: tiredness, listlessness, and finally loss of hair.

'I know you're never cured of cancer,' she said later, 'but I've got the all clear and I feel healthier than I ever did. I never used to have much of an appetite, but now I actually enjoy going out for a meal. I even have a glass of sherry.'

She enjoyed the support of friends during her recovery.

One night when the British Prime Minister, John Major, rang, Albert handed the phone to Kathleen. Mr Major told her that she was in both his and Norma's prayers every day.

The Majors, she says, are a very natural couple. They got along very well together when Albert, as Minister for Finance, had hosted his EC colleagues, including the Majors, for a weekend in Ashford Castle in 1990. John and Norma Major returned the hospitality with an immediate invite to their country residence.

'They show us pictures of their kids and we show them our lot,' said Kathleen.

On 29 December, 1990, the Reynolds' eldest daughter, Miriam, married a Tipperary man, Niall Fogarty from Carrick-on-Suir. Politicians were in the main absent from the glamorous wedding in Dublin's University Church on St Stephen's Green. But the well-known faces included Senator Donie Cassidy, publican Dessie Hynes, impressario Oliver Barry and Michael Smurfit. Meat baron Larry Goodman and his wife, Kitty, made an appearance at the reception. Old friend from the ballroom days, Paddy Cole, provided the music.

According to one report Emer and Leonie 'dazzled all and sundry in their off-shoulder canary yellow gowns from Marian Gale,' while youngest daughter Andrea performed as a soloist for the service.

Miriam, then aged twenty-seven and a solicitor, moved to Edinburgh where she now works along with her husband Niall, a chartered accountant.

A year previously Philip Reynolds, Managing Director of C&D Foods, married Anne Farrell from Westport, Co Mayo.

Having left the Cistercian College in Roscrea, he studied for an Irish Management Degree in Business Administration before joining the family firm.

In 1991 Phil and Anne Reynolds hit the headlines when local residents objected to the opening of a crèche at number 18A St Mary's Road in Ballsbridge. They later succeeded in securing permission for the crèche nearby at No 1A Wellington Road. The premises formerly belonged to kidnap victim, Dr John O'Grady.

In December 1990 Albert and Kathleen became grandparents when Anne gave birth to a son, Robert.

Having left secondary school Emer Reynolds studied for a BA at UCD before considering emigrating to Australia.

In an interview at the time her mother Kathleen said: 'If she goes it will break my heart, but I wouldn't stop her.'

As it happened Kathleen need not have worried, and Emer now works as a management consultant with the accountancy firm Price Waterhouse. She lives in an apartment in the Mespil Road complex in Dublin 4.

Leonie Reynolds also took a degree in UCD before studying at the King's Inns. Both Albert and Kathleen were present in the Supreme Court on 15 October, 1993, when she was called to the Bar by the Chief Justice, Tom Finlay. After qualifying she devilled at the Bar with barrister Richard Keane, a nephew of Chief Justice, Liam Hamilton. She also bought one of the Irish Life apartments in the Mespil complex.

Albert Reynolds Junior left Ireland for the United States after he graduated from UCD with a BA in November 1990. In the summer of that year he had worked on the trading floor of the Futures Exchange in Chicago, and developed an interest in investment banking. He now works with Chase Manhattan Bank in New York.

Cathy Reynolds graduated from UCD with a degree in politics and economics in 1992 and went to work in the European Commission in Brussels, while youngest daughter Andrea is studying pure economics.

While all have been active during election campaigns, none of them has yet shown an inclination to follow in their father's footsteps.

'We were never pressurised to be any more active in the party than we wanted to be, but we all campaign and I think we enjoy it,' said Leonie.

Commenting on speculation in 1987 that Albert might be the next Taoiseach, Kathleen commented: 'I wouldn't wish the job of Taoiseach on any man, but I wouldn't want to be selfish in holding him back . . . I know Albert is ambitious but he never told me he wanted to be Taoiseach, and I think he would prefer a ministry in the industry line'.

As wife of the Taoiseach, Kathleen Reynolds' dress sense is keenly noted at home and abroad. On visits abroad her choice of dress receives the same media attention as that of the President, Mary Robinson.

'Kathleen Reynolds is noteworthy for the simple reason that not many women of her age manage to slip into a size 10,' wrote Kathy Sheridan in *The Irish Times*. 'This, allied to the fact that she feels comfortable in short skirts, enables her to choose clothes for impact rather than camouflage.'

'Glamorous' is a word often used to describe her look. Her deep tan, along with that of Albert's, has become something of a trademark. They never appear to tire of the sun. Legend has it that Kathleen was born with a tan, and happy days working on the bog in her native Sligo merely enhanced it.

While she likes to wear a broad range of outfits, she is a regular supporter of Irish designers.

Paul Costello appeals to her for the more formal, tailored look, usually in strong colours.

She also likes Pat Crowley and her shopping sprees also take in Pia Bang, Marian Gale and Richard Alan.

The hand of Ian Galvin, a buyer for Brown Thomas, is also discernible from time to time.

But what is most obvious from a visit to the Reynolds home is the sense of boundless energy and good humour which radiates from Kathleen and her daughters.

Her doctors have warned her that there will be the odd week when she won't feel great.

'But,' she typically added, 'that's a very small price to pay for being alive.'

St Rita has stood by Kathleen Reynolds every time.

– 13 –
Albert The Survivor

'Mellow the moonlight to shine is beginning;
Close by the window young Eileen is spinning;
Bent o'er the fire her blind grandmother's sitting,
Is crooning and moaning and drowsily knitting....'

Government Press Secretary Seán Duignan was sitting in his office in Government Buildings on Dublin's Merrion Street slowly turning a hand-carved spinning wheel. The wheel, a gift delivered to the Taoiseach by Donegal South West Fianna Fáil Deputy, Mary Coughlan, in the summer of 1994, was placed in Seán Duignan's office.

When in a devilish mood the chief Government spin-doctor likes to 'spin' the wheel while singing the lyrics of the old Delia Murphy ballad.

Duignan was one of the new faces whom Albert Reynolds had appointed when he became Taoiseach in 1992.

A former RTE political correspondent, his charismatic personality was largely responsible for the success of the *Six-One* evening news programme. There his most memorable interview was, ironically, with Gerry Collins when, in a tearful plea, he begged Albert Reynolds not to 'burst the party' in the heave against Charles Haughey in November 1991.

Before that, along with Mike Burns and Kevin Healy, Duignan had pioneered the RTE *This Week* and *News at 1.30* radio programmes.

Duignan was then, and still is, a mercenary, willing to work for whoever makes him the best offer, although his father was a Fianna Fáil TD for Galway West in the late 1950s.

Duignan, or 'Diggie' as he is known in Leinster House, fashioned a new broadcast style of journalism, whereby he managed to buttonhole the viewer and cleverly slip a coded message across.

His style is typified by one story which he regularly tells friends.

During one heave against Charles Haughey in the early 1980s Duignan had broadcast an inconclusive piece with great style and conviction. The following day while in a pub on his way to Galway a man walked up to him and said: 'You could hear a pin drop here when you were on the box last night. We all agreed that you knew something, but you were saying nothing.'

Now appointed Government Press Secretary, Duignan argues that his job is not central, that he is in many ways peripheral to the goings-on in Government.

But most observers would argue that far from being peripheral, his role in Government Buildings is crucial.

On the night of Friday, 29 August, 1994, Seán Duignan was in the office of the Taoiseach, Albert Reynolds, awaiting the arrival of a copy of the Beef Tribunal report. There, too, was a team of legal advisers along with his communications advisers, Tom Savage and Donal Cronin of Carr Communications.

Earlier in the evening, shortly after 7.00 pm, the Minister for Agriculture, Joe Walsh, accompanied by the Secretary of the Department, Michael Dowling, had travelled to Dublin Castle to collect the long-awaited report.

The chairman of the Tribunal, Mr Justice Liam Hamilton, handed over a single copy of the report along with a master copy on computer disk. The disk proved incompatible with the Government printers' equipment and so the Taoiseach had to wait while the 1,074 page document was photocopied. It arrived in his office shortly after 9.00 pm where the document was divided up into sections for specialised analysis.

Shortly before 10.00 pm Albert Reynolds arrived to be briefed.

His advisers quickly assured him that he had been exonerated by the chairman from all the allegations of political favouritism made against him in relation to export credit insurance and had acknowledged that he had acted in the national interest.

The Taoiseach could scarcely contain his excitement and instructed Seán Duignan to inform the media that he was in the clear.

A hesitant Duignan questioned whether it was certain that this was the case. Selected quotations were shown to Duignan, who agreed to do as he was bid, but insisted he should first tell the Labour Party. He spoke by telephone to both Fergus Finlay and John Foley who advised against this course as Labour had not yet received a copy of the report.

Duignan went ahead and by his actions opened up one of the most serious rifts between Fianna Fáil and Labour since the formation of the partnership Government.

A question mark was placed over the action of the Government Press Secretary, but he had no apology to make.

'If I'm cast as the villain of the piece, I have no problem with that. It goes with the job,' he told *The Irish Times* political reporter Deaglán de Bréadún. 'The bottom line is I work for the Taoiseach, and I carry out his instructions.'

The selective leak and subsequent publication of the Beef Tribunal report brought to an end the State's longest and most expensive public enquiry.

Central to the Tribunal was the Goodman meat group and its activities.

When Fianna Fáil returned to power in 1987, within a month Larry Goodman had been offered export credit insurance – a State guarantee to pay up in the event of default by the purchasing country – to Iraq. The scheme had been suspended by the previous Fine Gael/Labour Government because of advice that the risks were too high in a country which was at war with its neighbour, Iran.

The multi-million pound insurance cover was given to Goodman by the then Minister for Industry and Commerce, Albert Reynolds.

Larry Goodman was also involved in a proposed 660 job expansion plan of his business. Despite objections from the Department of Finance that there was over capacity in the meat industry, a multi-million investment package was agreed, and publicly launched. The plan never materialised although the Goodman group did draw down some of the cheap loans which were agreed in association with discussions on the expansion.

As the State's insurance cover rose from £10,000,000 in April 1987 to £250,000,000 in 1988, a whole series of Dáil questions about activities in the Goodman Group began to arise.

Questions by the leader of the Progressive Democrats, Des O'Malley, established that the State's exposure for export credit insurance for beef sales exceeded the actual amount of exports. It later emerged that 38 per cent of the Goodman 'exports' came from Northern Ireland or Britain.

Finally, following further claims made in a BBC *World in Action* programme, the Beef Tribunal was set up in May 1991.

Described by *Irish Independent* agriculture correspondent Willie Dillon as the 'Frankenstein of Irish politics', it became a monster which grew horribly out of control, devouring the very Government that created it.

The enquiry took oral evidence from 459 witnesses during 226 days of hearings between October 1991 and July 1993. The testimony related to 142 allegations which were read out on the opening day of the Tribunal which had a sole member, Mr Justice Liam Hamilton.

The main subjects covered by the allegations were:
* Political favouritism: Politicians Dick Spring, Pat Rabbitte, Des O'Malley, Barry Desmond and others, had all made allegations that the Goodman Group was given special treatment in the allocation of export credit insurance, and changes in company taxation.

* Fraud in Irish beef plants, mainly in those owed by the Goodman group.
* Delayed investigations and cover-ups by the Department of Agriculture.
* Tax evasion: These allegations, raised and backed up by Pat Rabbitte, were not contested by the Goodman Group, and at time of writing at least £4,000,000 has been paid to the Revenue Commissioners.
* Political pressure: It was claimed that the IDA was pressurised by Fianna Fáil Ministers into making a rushed decision on a £90,000,000 investment package.
* Export credit insurance: The 1987-89 Government had re-introduced the insurance against the advice of officials. Des O'Malley claimed that the provision of State-backed insurance cover for non-Republic beef amounted to a fraud on the taxpayer.

Albert Reynolds was the key figure in the Beef Tribunal because he was the man responsible for granting credit insurance during the critical March 1987 to November 1988 period.

Some of his sworn evidence to the Tribunal was directly contradicted by other sworn evidence.

There was a conflict between Albert Reynolds and the evidence given by civil servants about decisions taken and instructions given at a crucial meeting in October 1988, and there was a contradiction between claims by Albert Reynolds that he did not know that much of the beef involved was from intervention stocks and notes of an interview he gave to *Sunday Tribune* journalist Rory Godson in which he allegedly accepted that he knew this.

There was also the political significance of his claim in evidence that Des O'Malley had knowingly misled the Tribunal on the subject of Goodman's claims for damages. That claim caused the downfall of the Fianna Fáil/PD Coalition Government in 1992.

Much attention centred on how the chairman of the Tribunal would deal with Labour Party leader Dick Spring's charge that by going against all available advice, a 'virtual monopoly' on insurance was given to Larry Goodman.

Spring accused Reynolds of having 'seriously neglected the national interest and damaged the industry as a whole in the process'. He also claimed that Reynolds' decisions were influenced by 'personal contacts' with 'persons in the beef industry'.

Spring further alleged that Larry Goodman had 'exceptional access' to Ministers, including Albert Reynolds, and that the Government, of which Reynolds was part, 'covered up illegal and improper activities in the beef industry since 1987'.

These were very serious charges. Any vindication of Spring, now Tánaiste in a Reynolds' Government, would have serious implications for the Government's future, while their rejection would be politically embarrassing for Spring.

However, an appeal to the Supreme Court which upheld Cabinet confidentiality ensured that the full facts of the decisions made at Cabinet meetings would never be revealed. That decision saved Albert Reynolds from major potential embarrassment.

The report, when it was finally published, was disappointing and an anti-climax.

In a skilfully written document, Liam Hamilton avoided pointing the finger directly at any one individual.

But the manner in which selected quotations were leaked by Seán Duignan late on Friday night, 29 July, caused major controversy.

In the days running up to the handing over of the report, Government spokesmen had informed political correspondents in Leinster House that the report would be studied over the weekend, following which there would be an early Cabinet meeting. That meeting would decide when the Dáil should be recalled.

But shortly before Friday midnight Seán Duignan rang around the newsrooms claiming the Taoiseach had been 'totally vindicated'. This, he said, was based on a 'preliminary assessment' of the section of the report on export credit insurance.

To back up his claim Mr Duignan cited two direct quotations from the report.

The first was: 'The determination of where the national interest lay was a matter for decision by the Minister for Industry and Commerce . . . the basis for those decisions was that they were in the national interest and the determination of the requirements of the national interest in these matters is a matter for the Minister for Industry and Commerce.'

Seán Duignan did not give the lines that separated the two parts of the quote. Later it emerged that there were in fact thirty-one pages of text in between.

The second extract was: 'There was no evidence to suggest that either the Taoiseach at any time or the Minister for Industry and Commerce was personally close to Mr Goodman or that Mr Goodman had any political associations with either of them or the party they represent . . . it is clear that he (Mr Goodman) had similar access to the previous Taoiseach, Dr FitzGerald, and members of his Government.'

Within a quarter of an hour of the statement being issued, the Tánaiste Dick Spring, in a highly unusual move, telephoned *The Irish Times* to say that the briefing given by Seán Duignan did not represent his views or those of the Government collectively.

'If Mr Duignan is purporting to act on behalf of the Government, he is not acting on my behalf and it must be a misunderstanding by him,' he added.

Seán Duignan quickly withdrew his earlier comments and said that 'in this instance I am a spokesman on behalf of the Taoiseach'.

The bizarre late night exchanges brought relations between Fianna Fáil and Labour to a new low in the Partnership Government. But they spoke volumes about Albert Reynolds and his keen instinct for survival.

'The Taoiseach's spin on the Beef Tribunal report provides a further example of a style of microphone politics that is vintage Reynolds,' wrote John Cooney in the *Irish Press*. 'This was the performance of a Taoiseach who is confident that within government he has gained the upper hand over Dick Spring's Labour Party.'

When the report was officially published on Tuesday, 2 August, it was far less upbeat than Duignan's leak suggested.

While the chairman accepted that the Minister for Industry and Commerce and the national Government were entitled to make decisions 'in the national interest', Mr Justice Hamilton also found that 'the national interest' would appear to require that before exposing the State to a potential liability of £1,000,000, a more detailed investigation of the benefits to the economy should have been carried out.

Such an investigation, if it had been carried out, would have found that a large portion of the beef to be exported was to be sourced outside the State, and much of it from intervention stocks. The chairman concluded that the benefits from such exports were 'illusory rather than real'.

Tánaiste Dick Spring, in a strongly worded statement, said the decisions taken to grant large amounts of export credit insurance 'turned out to be a policy disaster'.

Irish Times columnist, Fintan O'Toole, wrote that the findings of the report seriously undermined Albert Reynolds' claim that he had been fully vindicated.

'Mr Reynolds is entirely cleared of any suspicion that he acted for any motives other than "his conception of the requirements of the national interest". But the report also finds that his decisions were not in fact in the national interest, and that he failed to act in the manner which the national interest would appear to require,' wrote O'Toole.

The report, did, however, accept Albert Reynolds' evidence that he did not know that most of the beef was coming from intervention, a point which had been challenged by *Sunday Tribune* journalist Rory Godson.

The chairman also decided favourably for Albert Reynolds over a controversial letter from Larry Goodman to the Department of Industry and Commerce in November 1987.

A senior Department official, Joe Timbs, had given evidence that he had been given this letter by Mr Reynolds. The chairman found that 'Mr Timbs' account is mistaken, possibly due to faulty recollection'.

In other serious issues the chairman upheld the evidence of the officials.

There was conflict concerning a crucial meeting in the Department on 21 October, 1988, at which new allocations of export credit insurance were discussed. At the meeting Mr Reynolds announced that a Cabinet meeting held the previous June agreed that he could make new allocations. When the officials pointed out that this was not the case, Mr Reynolds undertook to seek clarification. There was conflict as to whether he ever sought the clarification before making decisions on new allocations.

According to Mr Reynolds himself, he did not make any decisions, but merely expressed views as to what the appropriate allocations would be after the matter was clarified. But the chairman found that 'pending clarification of this matter, the Minister for Industry and Commerce decided that the following additional cover would be provided for the Iraqi market . . .'

This finding suggested that Mr Reynolds went ahead and made decisions before he clarified the confusion surrounding a previous Cabinet meeting.

The report also contradicted claims made by Albert Reynolds in May 1991 surrounding the exclusion of another meat company, Halal, from securing export credit insurance.

Mr Reynolds claimed that Halal did not have a contract, which he claimed was fundamental for the granting of export credit insurance.

But the chairman found that before receiving an offer of insurance 'neither AIBP (Goodman) nor Hibernia Meats were required by the Minister for Industry and Commerce to produce confirmation of an executed contract for the sale of beef to the Iraqi authorities, whereas other beef exporters were so required'.

Although the report did not comment on particular allegations which were matters of opinion, it did in general uphold the claims made by Dick Spring against Albert Reynolds.

The overall trend of the report vindicated both Mr Reynolds and Mr Spring, but cast a dark cloud over their ability to remain in government together. In the event no Cabinet meeting took place and both men only spoke briefly twice before Mr Reynolds departed for a Mediterranean holiday.

Former Government Press Secretary PJ Mara warned that the antics of each of the parties in Government were damaging.

'The perception of their performance by the public in many ways has more influence than the actual delivery of the programme itself,' he said.

And he warned that the Reynolds' ploy of getting his say in first was outdated: '. . . the idea that whoever gets their claim in first, that that will last – that's not the way it works anymore'.

In July a senior Labour Party adviser had told the *Sunday Business Post* that the party was prepared to leave Government if Liam Hamilton described Albert Reynolds' actions as 'irresponsible' or 'inexplicable'. He used neither word, but his comments on Reynolds' handling of export credit insurance left him open to very serious criticism.

'If the findings were white, there would be no problem,' wrote Geraldine Kennedy, Political Correspondent of *The Irish Times*. 'If the findings were black, Labour would know that it had to pursue a certain course of action and leave the Government. But if the findings were grey, they would never get it right . . . The Tribunal's report is a dark shade of grey and could mark a watershed in the life of this Government.'

As the Dáil prepared for a three day debate on the report at the end of August, an MRBI poll in *The Irish Times* found that only 26 per cent of the public believed that Albert Reynolds had been cleared by the findings. The poll also revealed that the Taoiseach's own popularity rating had dropped 16 per centage points in six months. Fianna Fáil's own rating was down three points to 42 per cent.

The Dáil debate, which eventually took place on 1, 2, and 3 September, was completely overshadowed by the IRA ceasefire which took effect from midnight, 31 August. There was widespread speculation that the debate was arranged in the full knowledge of a likely ceasefire on that date.

'Admirers of "Albert the Survivor" winked and nodded at his astuteness and cuteness, while others just put it down to his legendary good luck and great sense of timing,' wrote 'Drapier' in *The Irish Times*.

The futility of the debate was shown on the opening morning when the Dáil rejected an Opposition demand that the Taoiseach and the Minister for Agriculture answer questions on the report. Mr Reynolds himself also stated that questions arising from the report would not be answered:

'Let me repeat it – this Tribunal is over. There are no questions still to be answered. We have already had over three years of questions and answers at the Tribunal. We will not now have a tribunal of inquiry into the Tribunal's findings.'

In a thirty-three page script the Taoiseach insisted he had been 'fully and totally vindicated, both personally and as a Minister' by the Beef Tribunal report.

In a skilfully prepared speech Mr Reynolds filleted the report to find support for his actions and sometimes finding that task difficult, he dismissed the findings and drew his own conclusions. He also indulged in some high-class mud-slinging.

'My integrity has been vindicated. I have been cleared of the allegations made against me – allegations of malpractice and wrongdoing. They have not been backed up by evidence....

'...The public are interested in the bottom line, not in the minutiae that appear to be so riveting to a handful of commentators,' he said. He quoted Fine Gael Senator Shane Ross who had written that 'an unnecessary political trial has been held, and it was a costly one at that'.

Referring to his controversial decisions on the granting of export credit insurance Mr Reynolds said that the Taoiseach and Ministers were appointed to take decisions and initiatives on their own responsibility, taking account of advice, but not always following it. In granting cover for exports to Iraq, he said he had noted the fact that many other countries, such as France, West Germany and the United States, were strengthening their trading positions with that country.

'I am as prudent and cautious with taxpayers' money as I am with my own,' he added.

Concluding, he quoted former US President Lyndon Johnson saying: 'If you came to hear me talk about all the things wrong, you are going home sad, because there are some things wrong, but the things that are right outnumber them a great deal.'

He would never claim that all his decisions were correct, but on balance he had made far more good than bad decisions.

But there was embarrassment for Albert Reynolds a few hours after he delivered his speech when the Tánaiste and Labour leader Dick Spring bluntly said that the Taoiseach's selective leaking of the findings of the report had 'damaged trust'.

'He (the Taoiseach) knows that that action damaged trust. The Taoiseach knows that I am prepared to work to restore it, and I believe he is, too.'

But Spring warned: 'If delicate and sensitive situations are to be played for party or personal advantage, this Government will fail.'

The trust between the two parties was again severely tested a few weeks later in a major row over who should be appointed President of the High Court in succession to Liam Hamilton, who had been appointed Chief Justice.

Despite hard-hitting attacks from the Fine Gael leader John Bruton who described Albert Reynolds as not only unfit for the office of Taoiseach, but unfit for any senior public office, and other Opposition deputies, the Government won the Dáil division at the end of the debate by a comfortable majority of thirty-two votes. Albert Reynolds had survived.

'The only certain conclusion to be drawn from the Beef Tribunal debate is that Fianna Fáil and the Labour Party will continue in Government together, even if they have to grit their teeth slightly to do so,' wrote *The Irish Times* chief political correspondent, Denis Coghlan.

Democratic Left TD Pat Rabbitte says the findings of the Tribunal were disappointing for the public, mainly because clear conclusions were not drawn.

'I don't think the public appreciate that it was generally a fact-finding mission by the chairman,' he says.

Rabbitte argues that it is unclear whether it will have an effect on the longer term because there is a great deal of damaging evidence in the report on the record of Dáil Éireann.

'Albert Reynolds came out of the Tribunal badly,' says Rabbitte. 'Firstly, he presented a rehearsed, uneasy and sometimes incoherent presentation and image. He came across as a man who has scant regard for academic research or detailed analysis of issues that confronted him as a Minister. Whereas he comes out of the report with his personal integrity intact, his Ministerial competence and judgement have been seriously indicted.'

PD deputy and Senior Counsel Michael McDowell agrees.

'Albert Reynolds emerges from the report as a man who behaved extraordinarily incompetently. He took massive risks to favour Larry

Goodman and didn't take any of the steps which were necessary to protect the downside of their involvement. He didn't protect the Government from political interference and even his evidence was rejected on a few occasions by the Tribunal. He also dumped on his civil servants. The more I look at the report of the Tribunal, the more sure I am that he is unsuited for public office.'

McDowell insists that had the Progressive Democrats been in government with Fianna Fáil, they would have 'demanded Albert's head'.

After the Tribunal little appeared to have changed. There were some changes in the meat industry, but many of these would have come with CAP reform in any case. A few individuals, including ironically the journalist Susan O'Keeffe, whose investigation triggered the setting up of the Tribunal, faced prosecution, and a *Freedom of Information Act* was promised.

'People like myself, who try to seek accountability, have the sinking feeling that we are like condemned men scratching a message to posterity on the wall of our cell,' commented Michael McDowell.

Meanwhile, a confused and bored public was left puzzled as to why there had been a Tribunal in the first place, and why it had cost them an estimated £35,000,000. That question will dominate the conversations in the pubs around Ireland long after the Hamilton inquiry becomes a dusty relic on the library shelves. Or, in the words of Chris Dooley, agriculture correspondent of the *Irish Press*: 'What, er, was it all about?'

– 14 –
Listen For The Angelus Bell

On 7 March, 1992, Albert Reynolds promised a new beginning.

Addressing his first Árd Fheis as Taoiseach and leader of Fianna Fáil he said the party would have a modern and open style aimed at single party Government after the next general election.

'I have one single overriding aim, and I want this party to share it. That aim is single party government.'

Albert Reynolds was not going to allow anybody to think that Fianna Fáil needed another party to keep it on the right track.

In selecting his Cabinet, he said he had not chosen people who would agree with each other all the time, and they had proved him right.

He promised the highest standards in public life.

'The future is also about fair dealing. No inside tracks, no privileged circles. The same rules should apply to everyone and the rewards should go to energy, hard work and professionalism.'

On social reform Albert Reynolds said Fianna Fáil had always been and would continue to be, associated with respect for family life, but in a modern democratic state the Government could not function as a paternal authority seeking to control the decisions of its citizens relative to personal morality.

Listening to Albert Reynolds, a discreet five seats away from the centre of the rostrum, was his predecessor, Charles Haughey. The handlers had placed him on the left so that when Albert entered from the right onto the stage he would neither have to ignore him nor shake hands with him. (Haughey refused to attend the 1993 Árd

Fheis when he discovered that he was consigned to sit with the Diplomatic Corps at the rear of the RDS hall.)

To show that this was the beginning of a new era, Albert Reynolds had a surprise in store.

'Since I became Taoiseach one small thing has bothered me every day that I've arrived at my office. The great gates of Government Buildings swing slowly behind me. I see people walking by, looking in. Looking in but not allowed to come in. I would like to change that . . .'

From the following June Government Buildings were to be open to the public every Saturday.

Albert Reynolds had been thrown into a Coalition Government at the deep end. The potential trouble that lay ahead was epitomised by the message he received from the Attorney General on his first day in office. Harry Whelehan had referred a case, in which a young pregnant girl wished to leave the country to have an abortion, to the High Court. The subsequent major controversy, known as the *X Case*, resulted in a three-way Referendum in November 1992.

But the Taoiseach had some immediate success with the passage of the Maastricht referendum in June 1992.

Behind the scenes all was not well between Fianna Fáil and their Government partners. Albert Reynolds began a practice of holding meetings between Fianna Fáil Ministers prior to Cabinet meetings to decide tactics.

In September, PD leader Des O'Malley wrote to the Taoiseach to protest at the departure from Cabinet proceedings through an emerging pattern of non-consultation. Throughout the autumn of 1992 the Cabinet barely hung together.

The final straw snapped during the Beef Tribunal when Albert Reynolds accused his Cabinet colleague, Des O'Malley, of being 'dishonest' concerning the amount of money owed to the Exchequer under the terms of the export credit insurance scheme.

A Motion of 'No Confidence' tabled by Fine Gael brought down the Government on 5 November.

In a sharp and scathing speech the Labour Party leader Dick Spring singled out Albert Reynolds for particular attack.

'This is the Taoiseach who preaches about respect for the institutions of this House, but who has lost the ability to conduct himself with dignity in any crisis.

'This is the Taoiseach who promised open Government, but whose Government fought in the Supreme Court to establish a system of Cabinet secrecy that flies in the face of that promise.

'This is the Taoiseach who talks about consensus, but who governs behind closed doors . . .'

Nine weeks later Dick Spring was in coalition with Albert Reynolds.

The November 1992 general election was a disaster for Fianna Fáil and its leader, Albert Reynolds. The campaign was uninspiring and the party lost nine Dáil seats. Its strength was reduced to sixty-eight deputies, thirteen short of an overall majority.

Albert Reynolds' dream had collapsed on his first attempt.

The battle was lost in Dublin where Fianna Fáil now controlled less than 33 per cent of the first preference vote. Senior colleagues urged Reynolds to go into Opposition but, ever a gambler, he hung on.

Fianna Fáil's losses were matched by Labour's gains where Dick Spring had more than doubled his number of Dáil seats.

For a time it looked as though Albert Reynolds might be the shortest leader of Fianna Fáil in history.

But luck was again at hand.

Two factors, the failure of the alternative Rainbow Coalition to agree among themselves, and the Taoiseach's claim that he had secured £8 billion at the EU December summit in Edinburgh, saw Fianna Fáil and Labour unite in an historic partnership government. The claim of £8 billion was later proved inaccurate with the real figure closer to £6 billion.

Resurrection is not too strong a word for Reynolds' comeback. Realising that few get a second chance, he grabbed it. In typical

Reynolds' style he waited until all the others had talked themselves to a standstill. Then he moved in.

The early days of the new Government were characterised by considerable confusion over responsibility, but it quickly got round to implementing a number of key reforms in the social area, including the easing of the law on the availability of condoms and the decriminalising of homosexuality. Other reforms, including divorce and the introduction of legislation to take account of the Supreme Court ruling in the *X Case*, have proved more difficult.

But it was the search for a solution to the Northern conflict that was to increasingly dominate Albert Reynolds' life as Taoiseach.

Albert Reynolds showed little interest in the North before he became Taoiseach.

Apart from attending the Arms Trial in 1970, he rarely spoke publicly on the issue at all. However, when questioned about this he insists that he was always aware of the North as he was born thirty-five miles from the Border. He also promoted dances in his early days in 'the Ulster Hall, in Caproni's in Bangor, in the Orpheus in Belfast, and in the Gap in Omagh, run by the former Bishop of Derry, Ned Daly'.

Reynolds also had business contacts with Northern Protestants through C&D Foods.

In 1985 he broke with Charles Haughey's opposition to the Anglo-Irish Agreement and told RTE that Fianna Fáil would support it in government.

'I remember the day well,' *News at 1.30* presenter Mike Burns recalls. 'I was ringing around all the Fianna Fáil people, and nobody would comment. I was at the end of my tether when I got Albert Reynolds at his home in Longford. He told me Fianna Fáil had always honoured international agreements.'

In one speech in Cork, in November 1989, Reynolds expressed the hope that the disappearance of barriers across Europe would have an effect on the Border.

'Surely,' he said, 'the historic animosities that have divided the people of this island and the two communities in the North are also amenable to these winds of change.'

In the early days of C&D Foods marketing manager Norman Spence can recall Albert Reynolds telling him the Provisional IRA would stop all violence if there was a declaration of intent by the British Government to reunite Ireland.

'The politicians and the businessmen in the North will run this country because they are better politicians than we are, and better businessmen than we are,' he told Spence.

The fact that he came to the complex Northern topic with an open mind, allowed him and British Prime Minister John Major to venture into new uncharted waters that were out of the reach of Charles Haughey and Margaret Thatcher.

Reynolds often pointed out that he and the British Prime Minister were 'two of a kind'.

John Major had also left school as a young man and went to work when he saw his father's business collapse.

Both men had always got on well together. In 1990, during Ireland's Presidency of the EC, the then Finance Minister Albert Reynolds asked John Major how he should portray the British position at a press conference.

'You run ahead and I will trot behind,' replied the Chancellor of the Exchequer.

Albert Reynolds and John Major are as unlike their predecessors Charles Haughey and Margaret Thatcher as it is possible to be.

'Whereas Haughey and Thatcher had buckets of charisma and the image of being "hard" personalities and "strong" leaders, Reynolds and Major by contrast are colourless men with "soft" public profiles,' wrote TP O'Mahony in the *Cork Examiner*.

Ever since the Arms Trial, Charles Haughey was carrying a lot of 'green' baggage, and was unable to win the confidence of the Unionist community.

Mrs Thatcher, on the other hand, was a hate figure to the IRA, especially since the H-Block hunger strikes in 1981.

Unexpectedly, Taoiseach Albert Reynolds turned himself into a good plain-English communicator on the Northern question.

'Colleagues joke that he cannot pass a microphone without talking to it, but this has become an asset as he has tirelessly laid down a barrage of high profile interviews in Dublin, and with the British and international media,' wrote Alan Murdoch in the *London Independent*.

But before Reynolds took over in Government, there were already major changes happening in the republican movement in the North.

Gerry Adams and Martin McGuinness had taken over Sinn Féin in the early '80s on a no-ceasefire basis. Adams quickly developed the organisation into an effective political machine which, in turn, led to a growing debate aimed at securing a lasting peace.

In 1988, in a heroic move that put his credibility at risk, the SDLP leader John Hume held a series of talks with Sinn Féin. The talks ended in stalemate, but an important marker had been put down.

The fact that Hume was prepared to talk to Adams also changed the climate of opinion in Washington, where an influential Irish-American group was playing a significant role in the search for peace.

Meanwhile, the campaign of violence continued.

In November 1989 the then Northern Ireland Secretary, Peter Brooke, drew the wrath of Unionists when he suggested a time might come when the British Government would talk to Sinn Féin. But most significantly of all, he said Britain had no selfish, strategic or economic interest in Northern Ireland. That remark laid the foundation stone for the Downing Street Declaration.

Brooke pursued a strategy of trying to bring all the constitutional parties to round-table talks, while at the same time privately wooing Republicans to give up violence.

In March 1991 he managed to get northern political parties, including Ian Paisley's Democratic Unionist Party, but minus Sinn

Féin, face to face with members of the Irish Government. Although these talks again ended in deadlock, it was a clear signal to Sinn Féin that they risked being left out in the cold.

Already there was a clear change in the thinking of Sinn Féin. Their policy document *Towards A Lasting Peace* specifically called on London and Dublin to seek agreement on the ending of partition. Traditionally Sinn Féin had regarded the Government in Dublin as a puppet administration. (In September 1994 following the ceasefire Gerry Adams referred to Albert Reynolds as 'The Boss'.)

When Albert Reynolds took over the leadership of Fianna Fáil in January 1992 he made peace in the North his priority.

He made this decision to pursue the peace process following a briefing from Charles Haughey when Haughey had lost office. However, he never consulted the former Taoiseach on the issue again.

After a British general election Sir Patrick Mayhew replaced Peter Brooke in Stormont.

In April 1992, with the assistance of SDLP leader John Hume and drawing on ideas put together over a lengthy period of time by Redemptorist priests Fr Alex Reid and Fr Gerry Reynolds in the Clonard Monastery in Belfast, Albert Reynolds drew up a first formal draft of a Joint Declaration to be made by the British and Irish Prime Ministers.

The two central principles of this document were a recognition by the British Government of the Irish people's right to self-determination, and a recognition by the Government of the Republic that this right could only be exercised with the agreement and consent of a majority of the people in Northern Ireland.

Playing a central role in the negotiations was Father Alex Reid. A native of Nenagh, Co Tipperary, he had also acted as a conduit for the Hume/Adams talks in 1988, the year he came to prominence when he was photographed giving the last rites to two British soldiers who were stripped, beaten and murdered after they had driven into the funeral of victims of the Milltown Cemetery attack. Speaking in the wake of that tragedy Fr Reid said: 'If the political authorities lived as closely to the situation and experienced its agony, they would get down to the roots of the problem much more quickly'.

A key player on the Irish Government side was a Tipperary Protestant, Dr Martin Mansergh, who was the principal speech writer on the North for Albert Reynolds. He also undertook a number of sensitive missions including secret journeys to the North.

In July 1992 Irish Government Ministers sat down in London with British Ministers and Unionist leaders. Later in the year members of the Ulster Unionist Party attended talks in Dublin Castle, but they broke down ahead of elections in the Republic.

In February 1993 the British Government received privately what it claimed was a message from the Provisional IRA saying that the conflict was over but it needed advice on how to bring it to an end. When these contacts became public Sinn Féin challenged this version, and insisted it was the British who initiated the contacts.

In April 1993 it leaked out that Gerry Adams and John Hume had resumed their contact. By September they had reached agreement, but both declined to publish the document they had agreed. Hume argued it had the potential to create peace.

Dublin reacted coolly to handling a document which had Gerry Adams' imprint. In the House of Commons, British Prime Minister John Major said the idea of talking to Mr Adams 'turned his stomach'.

And still the fighting continued.

In October a twenty-four-year-old, semi-literate North Belfast man, Thomas 'Bootsie' Begley, was sent by the IRA to bomb a shop in an attempt to kill loyalists upstairs. The device went off prematurely and ten Protestant men, women and children, along with Begley, were killed.

The loyalists exacted bitter revenge, machine-gunning six Catholics to death in a bar in Graysteel, Co Derry.

Then, when all seemed hopeless, a sudden populist push for peace saw renewed attempts by John Hume, who now moved centre stage.

There was a poignant moment when he attended a funeral in a Derry graveyard. The daughter of the assassinated man walked up to him and said: 'Mr Hume, we've just buried my father. My family wants you to know that when we said the Rosary around my daddy's coffin we prayed for you, for what you're trying to do to bring peace'. Hume shook the girl's hand, nodded and broke down in tears.

John Hume was under enormous pressure. He was chain-smoking, pale and not sleeping. In Strasbourg, attending a session of the European Parliament, as he tried to celebrate his birthday in a favourite restaurant he told this writer of the intense pressure he was under. But he was determined to see it through, he said, and was optimistic that peace could be achieved.

Early in November he collapsed and was taken to hospital suffering from exhaustion. During the following weeks he received 1,169 letters and get-well cards, urging him to press on.

In Dublin the Government adjusted its position, while in London a more reticent John Major also joined in the new drive for peace.

Negotiations intensified across the Irish Sea as position papers were reviewed and updated. The result was the Downing Street Declaration of December 15, 1993, which echoed the Hume/Adams document.

The final Declaration incorporated a number of recommendations which were received from loyalist unionists. The go-betweens were the Rev Roy Magee of the Presbyterian Church in Ireland congregation at Dundonald, Belfast, and Dublin trade unionist Chris Hudson, a founder member of the Peace Train Organisation. Reynolds told the Rev Magee to ask the loyalists to write down exactly what they wanted. Their response ended up, with a few minor changes, as Section Five of the Downing Street Declaration. It covered the rights of Unionists and made it at least partially acceptable to them.

The Downing Street Declaration marked a new watershed in Anglo-Irish relations and was widely welcomed as providing a basis for further negotiation. It offered Sinn Féin a place in political life if the IRA abandoned violence. There was also a promise by the Irish Government to set up a Forum for Peace and Reconciliation embracing all political parties north and south.

There was intense interest in the reaction of Sinn Féin.

Instead of outright rejection the party sought clarification on a number of clauses. The Dublin Government provided extensive clarification, but London initially declined. The Dublin Government also allowed Section 31 of the *Broadcasting Act*, long a source of frustration to Republicans, to lapse.

In February 1994, against the wishes of the British Government, Gerry Adams was granted a short-term visa to the United States where he received major publicity.

In April, the IRA declared a ceasefire, but it lasted only three days.

Now aged sixty-two, Albert Reynolds told a news conference in Washington in March that he would not see a united Ireland in his lifetime. However, this has not prevented him from outlining his personal vision of a new agreed Ireland in which he promised to give one-fifth of all Cabinet and senior Government posts to representatives from the North.

For him there was no turning back. The momentum for seeking peace could not be stopped.

In May the British Government finally issued a detailed clarification of the Declaration, but by then many believed the peace process was doomed.

In July, Sinn Féin finally gave its response to the Declaration at a conference in Letterkenny. It was widely interpreted by the media as negative.

However, rumours quickly spread that a substantial ceasefire was on the cards, with talk of a period of three months. While

Republicans had not accepted the Declaration, they were largely agreed that it was a realistic basis for further discussion.

All sides denied that there had been contacts with the British Government in the lead-up to the ceasefire, but it is likely that there were means of communication in existence.

In the week before the declaration of an IRA ceasefire the Irish/American group visited the North and conveyed assurances about additional International Fund monies from the US in the event of a permanent ceasefire. The Fund was contributing £19,000,000 a year, and this figure was expected to be trebled to £60,000,000 in the aftermath of the ceasefire.

The visits to Ireland by ex-Congressman Bruce Morrison, the Bill Clinton ally and friend from Yale University, were effectively that of a presidential envoy. In the twelve months before the September ceasefire he made three trips, meeting Sinn Féin, Unionist leaders, the Irish Government and Sir Patrick Mayhew.

Speaking on RTE on the eve of the ceasefire Albert Reynolds emphasised the influence of the Irish-Americans over the IRA. He said the last-minute decision to grant a visa to the former IRA leader Joe Cahill, and Sinn Féin Councillor Pat Treanor, was so important that there would have been no ceasefire announcement had it not occurred. Britain had advised against the visa being granted. It is understood that Cahill's role was to stand down the three active IRA units in the United States who provided arms and other supplies to the North.

On Monday night, 29 August, Albert Reynolds was given a draft copy of the IRA ceasefire statement by one of the Clonard priests. Reynolds and Spring agreed it was sufficient, despite the absence of the word 'permanent'.

'Listen out for the Angelus bell' was the cryptic message sent by the IRA to the Government on 31 August to alert them to the ceasefire announcement.

But the Government did not have to wait until twelve o'clock. Selected broadcast journalists, including RTE's special correspondent Charlie Bird, had been told to be at various points around Dublin where they were handed small packages wrapped in tissue. The packages contained a badly recorded tape-recording of a woman with a strong Northern accent reading the text of the IRA ceasefire statement, and a copy of the text itself.

RTE interrupted its scheduled programmes at 11.10 am to break the dramatic news.

The short statement promised 'a complete cessation of military operations' from midnight. It called on 'others, not least the British Government', to face up to their responsibilities.

For Albert Reynolds the news marked the high point in his political career, and gave him a place in history. He had succeeded where many before him had failed. He had achieved what a few years previously had seemed impossible. Nationally and internationally the former quiet Longford businessman was hailed as a hero.

In the Seanad long-time friend Senator Eddie Bohan while 'speaking on behalf of the people of North Longford including Ballinamuck and Drumlish,' said Albert Reynolds would 'go down in history along with people like Nelson Mandela, FW de Klerk, and President John F Kennedy for having achieved what nobody could have hoped to achieve.'

At its August session the European Parliament – with just one dissenting voice, that of Ian Paisley – nominated John Hume for the Nobel Peace Prize, in appreciation of his efforts.

'It's over, I don't care what words are used,' Albert Reynolds declared.

'It's the pinnacle of my career,' he told Olivia O'Leary in the *Sunday Tribune.*

'I have done the impossible because nobody ever thought it was possible,' he told Stephen Collins in the *Sunday Press.*

To mark the occasion the Taoiseach broke the pledge of a lifetime and sipped a glass of champagne – at the invitation of Tánaiste Dick Spring – with the members of his Cabinet.

The Fianna Fáil leader received two standing ovations when he attended a meeting of the Fianna Fáil Parliamentary Party in Leinster House. This was followed by a round of applause from all sides of the House when he and Tánaiste Dick Spring entered the Dáil at 4.30 pm.

Later he told reporters that he felt 'a quiet sense of achievement', particularly as some people had not seen him as somebody with strong credentials in the Republican ethos.

The Taoiseach said the Northern people were 'different' but they were very straight-talking.

'They have a lot more respect for you when you say what you mean – and I do that. I felt I could give it enough time and talk to as many people as possible. I could begin to knock barriers down.'

He assured the Unionist community that they had nothing to fear, and moved to allay worries from the British side about the absence of the word 'permanent' from the IRA statement.

Later, in a speech to the Dáil the Taoiseach recalled that at times he was almost alone, apart from his Government colleagues, in keeping faith in the possibility of peace.

'I knew that if I publicly wrote off the peace process, that would be universally regarded as the end,' he said.

He said that for over twenty years successive governments largely succeeded in protecting the stability of the State from attack. But the price of keeping a rigid distance from those involved in violence was that the State exercised little or no influence, other than a repressive one, on Republican thinking.

No one person or group could claim responsibility for the ceasefire, he told the Irish nation in a special televised address.

'It was earned, shaped and created by people who have suffered, people who have sympathised, people who have taken action to indicate that they wanted peace and would not settle for anything but peace.'

Peace, he said, was an open door for normality, for decency, and for rediscovering each other as human beings, not as stereotypes and enemies.

'I have,' he continued, 'been direct and unambiguous at all times throughout the years leading to this ceasefire and I am being direct and unambiguous now. There is no deal. There are no hidden agreements.'

'Is it over for good, Albert?' John Major asked Albert Reynolds on the telephone.

'Yes, John, it's over for good,' replied the Taoiseach.

Six weeks after the IRA ceasefire, on October 13, the loyalist paramilitary organsiations in the North also announced they would 'universally cease all operational hostilities'.

On Tuesday, 6 September, Albert Reynolds, John Hume and Gerry Adams shook hands together on the steps of Government Buildings. The handshake contrasted with the controversy which erupted over a year earlier when President Mary Robinson shook hands with the Sinn Féin leader in Whiterock Community College in West Belfast on 18 June 1993.

The meeting of Reynolds, Hume and Adams – the three faces of Irish nationalism – heralded the beginning of a new era 'totally and absolutely committed to democratic and peaceful methods of resolving our political problems'.

Adams greeted the Taoiseach in Irish before the three men spent over one hour in talks about the new political situation.

The historic meeting, criticised by the Unionists as being far too premature, cemented the IRA ceasefire and the opening of a new chapter in the attempt to resolve the Northern Ireland question.

****

So how important was Albert Reynolds' role in the ceasefire?

Historian and Fine Gael Senator Maurice Manning observes that the Fianna Fáil party has a great capacity in times of success to overact and go over the top.

'What we saw was a ceasefire, not a final settlement. Every Taoiseach up to now has been roughly where Albert Reynolds is now. Liam Cosgrave was there in Sunningdale. Charles Haughey was there in his talks when the totality of relationships was on the table. Garret FitzGerald was there with the Anglo-Irish Agreement. In each case progress was made, but it was slow and unspectacular.'

The key question now, says Manning, is whether the ceasefire is the dramatic breakthrough which Albert Reynolds represents it, or whether it is just one more step on the way forward. It is still far too early to tell.

Senator Manning pays tribute to Albert Reynolds for his tenacity.

'In the case of every other Taoiseach what happened would not have happened without their particular input. It's equally true in the case of Albert Reynolds. He has shown a persistence, a capacity to stay with something, and a belief in himself by pushing it as far as he has.'

Deputy Pat Rabbitte of Democratic Left argues that a key factor helping Reynolds was that he did not bring any baggage with him to the Northern issue.

'The achievement of a permanent cessation of violence, if that is what we have achieved, is an outstanding one,' he says. 'I would be the first to applaud if the Taoiseach was internationally recognised for that.'

Rabbitte adds that it must be a matter of some chagrin to the Taoiseach's two predecessors, Charles Haughey and Dr Garret FitzGerald, both of whom displayed a far deeper knowledge and understanding of Northern Ireland, that 'Albert should be the man in the gap'.

Lawyer and Progressive Democrat Dáil Deputy, Michael McDowell, is less enthusiastic. For him the IRA has not rejected violence permanently.

'What Sinn Féin wants is to transform the IRA into a kind of *gens d'armerie* for the Catholic community, and that is a recipe for disaster.'

Deputy McDowell argues that the IRA ceasefire is not central to the final settlement.

'Northern Ireland will remain part of the United Kingdom. There will be North/South institutions exercising executive functions with delegated responsibility in certain areas. There will be a power-sharing Assembly and there will be a revolution of the institutional system in the North to make it more Catholic-friendly. Even if the IRA do not want it, that is what will happen. I don't think the establishment of the ceasefire in advance of the settlement is crucial to the nature of the settlement. There will be no agreement put in place that will signify the end of the Union and the IRA must realise that.'

And what of Albert Reynolds' place in history?

Clearly it is still far too early to make a realistic assessment. But there are some yardsticks in place.

He will primarily be remembered as the man who was Taoiseach during the negotiations for peace in Northern Ireland, irrespective of the final outcome. Further success in this forum will enhance his reputation.

How much of the credit will go to Albert Reynolds is also unclear. For example, an opinion poll in the *Daily Telegraph* on 8 September showed 27 per cent of the people surveyed gave most credit to John Hume for halting hostilities, while 22 per cent named Gerry Adams. Only 18 per cent gave most credit to Albert Reynolds and 12 per cent named John Major.

'Most people would agree there were two or three great Taoisigh,' says Maurice Manning. 'Seán Lemass and WT Cosgrave were both constructive, quiet, non-flamboyant builders and reconcilers. So far with Albert Reynolds we see the achievement on Northern Ireland, and a great talent for survival in the most dramatic of circumstances.'

Michael McDowell's assessment is more blunt:

'When the history of the 20th century is written, Albert Reynolds will be looked on with indifference.'

In Albert Reynolds we have seen a Taoiseach who lost the confidence of the electorate in his only general election to date, failing dismally in his stated aim on his election to the leadership of Fianna Fáil – to win an overall majority for the party. His future was only saved by the failure of Fine Gael and Labour to work together in government where again he was extraordinarily lucky.

Albert Reynold's style of leadership has also been strongly criticised for his frequent trips abroad. One commentator branded his administration as 'the first Government-on-Tour, a sort of futuristic showband, forever on the move'.

Luck has favoured Albert Reynolds more than most throughout his career. Success in business has put his personal wealth at an estimated £3,000,000 to £4,000,000. From his timing to get in and out of ballrooms, to his selection as a Dáil candidate in 1977, to his persistence with the peace process, he has proved again and again his ability to grasp an opportunity and take it to its conclusion. Time and again he was the right man in the right place at the right time.

Will his luck run out?

Perhaps. Or will he achieve his final ambition, which some of those close to him say is to succeed Mary Robinson as President of Ireland?

Appendix 1

Downing Street Joint Declaration, 15 December, 1993

1. The Taoiseach, Mr Albert Reynolds TD, and the Prime Minister the Rt Hon John Major MP, acknowledge that the most urgent and important issue facing the people of Ireland, North and South, and the British and Irish Governments together, is to remove the causes of conflict, to overcome the legacy of history and to heal the divisions which have resulted, recognising that the absence of a lasting and satisfactory settlement of relationships between the peoples of both islands has contributed to continuing tragedy and suffering. They believe that the development of an agreed framework for peace, which has been discussed between them since early last year, and which is based on a number of key principles articulated by the two Governments over the past 20 years, together with the adaptation of other widely accepted principles, provides the starting point of a peace process designed to culminate in a political settlement.

2. The Taoiseach and the Prime Minister are convinced of the inestimable value to both their peoples, and particularly for the next generation, of healing divisions in Ireland and of ending a conflict which has been so manifestly to the detriment of all. Both recognise that the ending of divisions can come about only through the agreement and co-operation of the people, North and South, representing both traditions in Ireland. They therefore make a solemn commitment to promote co-operation at all levels on the basis of the fundamental principles, undertakings, obligations under international agreements, to

which they have jointly committed themselves, and the guarantees which each Government has given and now reaffirms, including Northern Ireland's statutory constitutional guarantee. It is their aim to foster agreement and reconciliation, leading to a new political framework founded on consent and encompassing arrangements within Northern Ireland, for the whole island, and between these islands.

3. They also consider that the development of Europe will, of itself, require new approaches to serve interests common to both parts of the island of Ireland, and to Ireland and the United Kingdom as partners in the European Union.

4. The Prime Minister, on behalf of the British Government, reaffirms that they will uphold the democratic wish of a greater number of the people of Northern Ireland on the issue of whether they prefer to support the Union or a sovereign united Ireland. On this basis, he reiterates, on behalf of the British Government, that they have no selfish strategic or economic interest in Northern Ireland. Their primary interest is to see peace, stability and reconciliation established by agreement among all the people who inhabit the island, and they will work together with the Irish Government to achieve such an agreement, which will embrace the totality of relationships. The role of the British Government will be to encourage, facilitate and enable the achievement of such agreement over a period through a process of dialogue and co-operation based on full respect for the rights and identities of both traditions in Ireland. They accept that such agreement may, as of right, take the form of agreed structures for the island as a whole, including a united Ireland achieved by peaceful means on the following basis. The British Government agree that it is for the people of the island of Ireland alone, by agreement between the two parts respectively, to exercise their right of self-

determination on the basis of consent, freely and concurrently given, North and South, to bring about a united Ireland, if that is their wish. They reaffirm as a binding obligation that they will, for their part, introduce the necessary legislation to give effect to this, or equally to any measure of agreement on future relationships in Ireland which the people living in Ireland may themselves freely so determine without external impediment. They believe that the people of Britain would wish, in friendship to all sides, to enable the people of Ireland to reach agreement on how they may live together in harmony and in partnership, with respect for their diverse traditions, and with full recognition of the special links and the unique relationship which exist between the peoples of Britain and Ireland.

5. The Taoiseach, on behalf of the Irish Government, considers that the lessons of Irish history, and especially of Northern Ireland, show that stability and well-being will not be found under any political system which is refused allegiance or rejected on grounds of identity by a significant minority of those governed by it. For this reason, it would be wrong to attempt to impose a united Ireland, in the absence of the freely given consent of a majority of the people of Northern Ireland. He accepts, on behalf of the Irish Government, that the democratic right of self-determination by the people of Ireland as a whole must be achieved and exercised with and subject to the agreement and consent of a majority of the people of Northern Ireland and must, consistent with justice and equity, respect the democratic dignity and the civil rights and religious liberties of both communities, including:
– the right of free political thought;
– the right to freedom and expression of religion;
– the right to pursue democratically national and political aspirations;

- the right to seek constitutional change by peaceful and legitimate means;
- the right to live wherever one chooses without hindrance;
- the right to equal opportunity in all social and economic activity, regardless of class, creed, sex or colour.

These would be reflected in any future political and constitutional arrangements emerging from a new and more broadly based agreement.

6. The Taoiseach however recognises the genuine difficulties and barriers to building relationships of trust either within or beyond Northern Ireland, from which both traditions suffer. He will work to create a new era of trust, in which suspicion of the motives or actions of others is removed on the part of either community. He considers that the future of the island depends on the nature of the relationship between the two main traditions that inhabit it. Every effort must be made to build a new sense of trust between those communities. In recognition of the fears of the Unionist community and as a token of his willingness to make a personal contribution to the building up of that necessary trust, the Taoiseach will examine with his colleagues any elements in the democratic life and organisation of the Irish State that can be represented to the Irish Government in the course of political dialogue as a real and substantial threat to their way of life and ethos, or that can be represented as not being fully consistent with a modern democratic and pluralist society, and undertakes to examine any possible ways of removing such obstacles. Such an examination would of course have due regard to the desire to preserve those inherited values that are largely shared throughout the island or that belong to the cultural and historical roots of the people of this island in all their diversity. The Taoiseach hopes that over time a meeting of hearts and

minds will develop, which will bring all the people of Ireland together, and will work towards that objective, but he pledges in the meantime that as a result of the efforts that will be made to build mutual confidence no Northern Unionist should ever have to fear in future that this ideal will be pursued either by threat or coercion.

7. Both Governments accept that Irish unity would be achieved only by those who favour this outcome persuading those who do not, peacefully and without coercion or violence, and that, if in the future a majority of the people of Northern Ireland are so persuaded, both Governments will support and give legislative effect to their wish. But, notwithstanding the solemn affirmation by both Governments in the Angle-Irish Agreement that any change in the status of Northern Ireland would only come about with the consent of a majority of the people of Northern Ireland, the Taoiseach also recognises the continuing uncertainties and misgivings which dominate so much of Northern Unionist attitudes towards the rest of Ireland. He believes that we stand at a stage of our history when the genuine feelings of all traditions in the North must be recognised and acknowledged. He appeals to both traditions at this time to grasp the opportunity for a fresh start and a new beginning, which could hold such promise for all our lives and the generations to come. He asks the people of Northern Ireland to look on the people of the Republic as friends, who share their grief and shame over all the suffering of the last quarter of a century, and who want to develop the best possible relationship with them, a relationship in which trust and new understanding can flourish and grow. The Taoiseach also acknowledges the presence in the Constitution of the Republic of elements which are deeply resented by Northern Unionists, but which at the same time reflect hopes and ideals which lie

deep in the hearts of many Irish men and women North and South. But as we move towards a new era of understanding in which new relationships of trust may grow and bring peace to the island of Ireland, the Taoiseach believes that the time has come to consider together how best the hopes and identities of all can be expressed in more balanced ways, which no longer engender division and the lack of trust to which he has referred. He confirms that, in the event of an overall settlement, the Irish Government will, as part of a balanced constitutional accommodation, put forward and support proposals for change in the Irish Constitution which would fully reflect the principle of consent in Northern Ireland.

8. The Taoiseach recognises the need to engage in dialogue which would address with honesty and integrity the fears of all traditions. But that dialogue, both within the North and between the people and their representatives of both parts of Ireland, must be entered into with an acknowledgement that the future security and welfare of the people of the island will depend on an open, frank and balanced approach to all the problems which for too long have caused division.

9. The British and Irish Governments will seek, along with the Northern Ireland constitutional parties through a process of political dialogue, to create institutions and structures which, while respecting the diversity of the people of Ireland, would enable them to work together in all areas of common interest. This will help over a period to build the trust necessary to end past divisions, leading to an agreed and peaceful future. Such structures would, of course, include institutional recognition of the special links that exist between the peoples of Britain and Ireland as part of the totality of relationships, while taking account of newly forged links with the rest of Europe.

10. The British and Irish Governments reiterate that the achievement of peace must involve a permanent end to the use of, or support for, paramilitary violence. They confirm that, in these circumstances, democratically mandated parties which establish a commitment to exclusively peaceful methods and which have shown that they abide by the democratic process, are free to participate fully in democratic politics and to join in dialogue in due course between the Governments and the political parties on the way ahead.

11. The Irish Government would make their own arrangements within their jurisdiction to enable democratic parties to consult together and share in dialogue about the political future. The Taoiseach's intention is that these arrangements could include the establishment, in consultation with other parties, of a Forum for Peace and Reconciliation to make recommendations on ways in which agreement and trust between both traditions in Ireland can be promoted and established.

12. The Taoiseach and the Prime Minister are determined to build on the fervent wish of both their peoples to see old fears and animosities replaced by a climate of peace. They believe the framework they have set out offers the people of Ireland, North and South, whatever their tradition, the basis to agree that from now on their differences can be negotiated and resolved exclusively by peaceful political means. They appeal to all concerned to grasp the opportunity for a new departure. That step would compromise no position or principle, nor prejudice the future for either community. On the contrary, it would be an incomparable gain for all. It would break decisively the cycle of violence and the intolerable suffering it entails for the people of these islands, particularly for both communities in Northern Ireland. It would allow the process of economic and social co-operation on the island to realise its full potential for

prosperity and mutual understanding. It would transform the prospects for building on the progress already made in the talks process, involving the two Governments and the constitutional parties in Northern Ireland. The Taoiseach and the Prime Minister believe that these arrangements offer an opportunity to lay the foundations for a more peaceful and harmonious future devoid of the violence and bitter divisions which have scarred the past generation. They commit themselves and their Governments to continue to work together, unremittingly, towards that objective.

Appendix 2
IRA Statement 3 August 1994

Recognising the potential of the current situation, in order to enhance the democratic peace process and to underline our definitive commitment to its success, the leadership of Óglaigh na hÉireann have decided that as of midnight Wednesday, August 31, there will be a complete cessation of military operations.

All our units have been instructed accordingly.

At this historic crossroads the leadership of Óglaigh na hÉireann salutes and commends the courage of our volunteers and other activists, our supporters and the political prisoners who have sustained this struggle against all odds for 25 years.

Your courage, determination and sacrifice have demonstrated that the spirit of freedom and the desire for peace, based on a just and lasting settlement cannot be crushed.

We remember all those who have died for Irish freedom and we reiterate our commitment to our republican objectives.

Our struggle has seen many gains and advances made by nationalists and for the democratic position.

We believe that an opportunity to secure a just and lasting settlement has been created.

We are therefore entering into a new situation in a spirit of determination and confidence. Determined that the injustices which created this conflict will be removed and confident in the strength and justice of our struggle to achieve this.

We note that the Downing Street Declaration is not a solution, nor was it presented as such by its authors. A solution will only be found as a result of inclusive negotiations.

Others, not least the British Government, have a duty to face up to their responsibilities. It is our desire to significantly contribute with energy, determination and patience.

Appendix 3

The following are the names of the Fianna Fáil TDs as they are believed to have voted for the three leadership candidates on February 6, 1992. The vote was by secret ballot.

For Albert Reynolds

Bertie Ahern (Dublin Central)
Dermot Ahern (Louth)
Michael Ahern (Cork East)
David Andrews (Dun Laoghaire)
Liam Aylward (Carlow Kilkenny)
Michael Barrett (Dublin North West)
Gerard Brady (Dublin South East)
Vincent Brady (Dublin North Central)
Matthew Brennan (Sligo Leitrim)
Seamus Brennan (Dublin South)
Ben Briscoe (Dublin South Central)
John Browne (Wexford)
Seán Calleary (Mayo East)
Ivor Callely (Dublin North Central)
Ger Connolly (Laois Offaly)
Mary Coughlan (Donegal South West)
Brian Cowen (Laois Offaly)

Brendan Daly (Clare)
Noel Davern (Tipperary South)
John Dennehy (Cork South Central)
Noel Dempsey (Meath)
Síle de Valera (Clare)
John Ellis (Sligo Leitrim)
Frank Fahey (Galway East)
Jackie Fahey (Waterford)
Dermot Fitzpatrick (Dublin Central)
Chris Flood (Dublin South West)
Pádraig Flynn (Mayo West)
Pat The Cope Gallagher (Donegal SW)
Maire Geoghegan-Quinn (Galway W)
Brian Hillery (Dun Laoghaire)
Liam Hyland (Laois Offaly)
Joe Jacob (Wicklow)
Laurence Kelly (Cork North West)
Brendan Kenneally (Waterford)
Seamus Kirk (Louth)
Michael Kitt (Galway East)

Tom Kitt (Dublin South)
Liam Lawlor (Dublin West)
Jimmy Leonard (Cavan Monaghan)
Terry Leyden (Roscommon)
Chris Lyons (Cork North Central)
Charlie McCreevy (Kildare)
Tom McEllistrim (Kerry North)
Micheál Martin (Cork South Central)
TJ Morley (Mayo East)
Michael Noonan (Limerick West)
John O'Connell (Dublin South Central)

William O'Dea (Limerick East)
Rory O'Hanlon (Cavan Monaghan)
Michael O'Kennedy (Tipperary North)
John O'Leary (Kerry South)
Seán Power (Kildare)
Albert Reynolds (Longford)
Dick Roche (Wicklow)
Michael Smith (Tipperary N)
Noel Treacy (Galway)
Jim Tunney (Dublin North West)
Dan Wallace (Cork NC)
Joe Walsh (Cork South West)
John Wilson (Cavan Monaghan)

For Michael Woods

Gerard Collins (Limerick West)
Seamus Cullimore (Wexford)
Liam Fitzgerald (Dublin North East)
Charles Haughey (Dublin North Central)
Colm Hilliard (Meath)
Jim McDaid (Donegal North East)
John O'Donoghue (Kerry South)
John Stafford (Dublin Central)
Mary Wallace (Meath)
Michael Woods (Dublin North East)

For Mary O'Rourke

Ray Burke (Dublin North)
Brian Lenihan (Dublin West)
M J Nolan (Carlow Kilkenny)
Ned O'Keeffe (Cork East)
Mary O'Rourke (Longford Westmeath)
Martin Joe O'Toole (Mayo West)

Bibliography

Browne, Vincent (Ed) (1981) *The Magill Book of Irish Politics*, Dublin: Magill Publications.

Browne, Vincent (Ed) (1982) *The Magill Guide to Election '82*, Dublin: Magill Publications.

Collins, Stephen (1992) *The Haughey File*, Dublin: The O'Brien Press.

Farrell, Michael (Ed) (1984) *Magill Book of Irish Politics 1984* Dublin: Magill Publications.

FitzGerald, Garret (1991) *All in a Life, An Autobiography*, Dublin: Gill and Macmillan.

Nealon, Ted (Ed) (1993) *Nealon's Guide to the 27th Dail & Seanad*, Dublin: Gill & Macmillan.

O'Mahony, TP (1991) *Jack Lynch, A Biography*, Dublin: Blackwater Press.

Oram, Hugh (1983) *Paper Tigers*, Dublin: Appletree Press.

Power, Vincent (1990) *Send 'em Home Sweatin'*, Dublin: Kildanore Press.

Ryan, Tim (1992) *Mara, PJ*, Dublin: Blackwater Press.

Trench, Brian (Ed) (1983) *Magill Book of Irish Politics 1983*, Dublin: Magill Publications.

Trench, Brian (Ed) (1987) *Magill Book of Irish Politics 1987*, Dublin: Magill Publications.

Walsh, Dick (1986) *The Party, Inside Fianna Fáil*, Dublin: Gill and Macmillan.

Index

O

O'Bradaigh, Ruadhri 100, 121
O'Brien, Brendan 21
O'Brien, Conor Cruise 104, 126
O'Carroll, Brian 80
O'Connell, John 160, 163
O'Dea, Jimmy 16, 96
O'Dea, Willie 160
O'Donnell, Brendan 109
O'Donnell, Daniel 32
O'Donoghue, District Justice Dinny 37
O'Donoghue, Eamon 162
O'Donoghue, Martin 113, 124, 125, 128, 130, 131
O'Grady, John 175
O'Hanlon, Rory 143
O'Hara, Peter 63
O'Keefe, Alan 93
O'Keefe, Batt 83
O'Keefe, Susan 191
O'Kennedy, Michael 75, 112, 131, 150
O'Leary, Olivia 203
O'Mahony, TP 196
O'Malley, Des 79, 96, 101, 102, 112, 119, 124, 125, 127, 128, 132, 146, 162, 181, 182, 193
O'Malley, Pat 142
O'Meara, Brendan 17
O'Morain, Michael 77
Oram, Hugh 89, 91
Orbison Roy 29
O'Reilly, Dr Colm 140
O'Rourke, Dan 5
O'Rourke, Jack 28
O'Rourke, Mary 123, 129, 130, 133, 134, 140, 145, 154, 160, 164
O'Toole Fintan 185

P

Paisley, Ian 197, 203
Pearse, Pádraig 111
Phelan, Angela 166
Power, Brenda 85, 166, 167
Power, Paddy 153
Power, Seán 152, 153

Power, Vincent 20, 21, 27, 32
Purcell, Deirdre 9, 32, 101, 105

Q

Quinn, Fergal 48, 57
Quinn, Maire Geoghegan 79, 115, 151, 155, 163
Quinn, Pat 25
Quinn, Ruairi 14

R

Rabbitte, Pat 80, 181, 182, 190, 206
Reeves, Jim 29
Reid, Eileen 21
Reid, Fr Alex 198, 199
Reilly, Ned 'The County' 2
Reynolds, Albert Jnr 76, 165, 169, 170
Reynolds, Andrea 114, 169, 170, 174, 176
Reynolds, Anne 34
Reynolds, Cathy 165, 169, 170, 173, 176
Reynolds, Charlie 5, 115
Reynolds, Emer 114, 133, 169, 170, 172, 174, 175
Reynolds, Fr Gerry 198
Reynolds, Gerry 161
Reynolds, Jim 4, 5, 12, 17, 22, 24, 25, 27, 29, 33, 35, 39, 81, 106, 138, 168
Reynolds, Joe 4, 5, 9, 10, 17, 33, 97, 115
Reynolds, John 34, 35
Reynolds, John P 4
Reynolds, Kathleen 3, 15, 34, 36, 52, 59, 62, 68, 73, 75, 76, 91, 111-113, 156, 162, 165-177
Reynolds, Leonie 174, 176
Reynolds, Miriam 114, 169, 174, 175
Reynolds, Peter 36
Reynolds, Philip 75, 76, 81, 84, 86, 169, 170, 174
Reynolds, Teresa 4, 5, 115
Reynolds, Leonie 169
Richard, Little 29
Riley, Phil 166
Robinson, Mary 163, 176, 205, 208
Rock, Dickie 21, 27